CISCO

Course Booklet

CCNA Discovery

Networking for Home and Small Businesses

Version 4.0

ciscopress.com

Cisco | Networking Academy
Mind Wide Open

CCNA Discovery Course Booklet Networking for Home and Small Businesses, Version 4.0

Cisco Networking Academy

Copyright© 2010 Cisco Systems, Inc.

Published by:
Cisco Press
800 East 96th Street
Indianapolis, IN 46240 USA

Printed in the United States of America

First Printing   October 2009

Library of Congress Cataloging-in-Publication Data is on file.

ISBN-13: 978-1-58713-242-1

ISBN-10: 1-58713-242-7

Warning and Disclaimer

This book is designed to provide information about Networking. Every effort has been made to make this book as complete and as accurate as possible, but no warranty or fitness is implied.

The information is provided on an "as is" basis. The authors, Cisco Press, and Cisco Systems, Inc. shall have neither liability nor responsibility to any person or entity with respect to any loss or damages arising from the information contained in this book or from the use of the discs or programs that may accompany it.

The opinions expressed in this book belong to the author and are not necessarily those of Cisco Systems, Inc.

Publisher
Paul Boger

Associate Publisher
Dave Dusthimer

Cisco Representative
Erik Ullanderson

**Cisco Press
Program Manager**
Anand Sundaram

Executive Editor
Mary Beth Ray

Managing Editor
Patrick Kanouse

Project Editor
Bethany Wall

Editorial Assistant
Vanessa Evans

Cover Designer
Louisa Adair

Composition
Mark Shirar

This book is part of the Cisco Networking Academy® series from Cisco Press. The products in this series support and complement the Cisco Networking Academy curriculum. If you are using this book outside the Networking Academy, then you are not preparing with a Cisco trained and authorized Networking Academy provider.

For more information on the Cisco Networking Academy or to locate a Networking Academy, Please visit www.cisco.com/edu.

CISCO.

Trademark Acknowledgments

All terms mentioned in this book that are known to be trademarks or service marks have been appropriately capitalized. Cisco Press or Cisco Systems, Inc., cannot attest to the accuracy of this information. Use of a term in this book should not be regarded as affecting the validity of any trademark or service mark.

Feedback Information

At Cisco Press, our goal is to create in-depth technical books of the highest quality and value. Each book is crafted with care and precision, undergoing rigorous development that involves the unique expertise of members from the professional technical community.

Readers' feedback is a natural continuation of this process. If you have any comments regarding how we could improve the quality of this book, or otherwise alter it to better suit your needs, you can contact us through email at feedback@ciscopress.com. Please make sure to include the book title and ISBN in your message.

We greatly appreciate your assistance.

Americas Headquarters
Cisco Systems, Inc.
San Jose, CA

Asia Pacific Headquarters
Cisco Systems (USA) Pte. Ltd.
Singapore

Europe Headquarters
Cisco Systems International BV
Amsterdam, The Netherlands

Cisco has more than 200 offices worldwide. Addresses, phone numbers, and fax numbers are listed on the Cisco Website at **www.cisco.com/go/offices.**

CCDE, CCENT, Cisco Eos, Cisco HealthPresence, the Cisco logo, Cisco Lumin, Cisco Nexus, Cisco StadiumVision, Cisco TelePresence, Cisco WebEx, DCE, and Welcome to the Human Network are trademarks; Changing the Way We Work, Live, Play, and Learn and Cisco Store are service marks; and Access Registrar, Aironet, AsyncOS, Bringing the Meeting To You, Catalyst, CCDA, CCDP, CCIE, CCIP, CCNA, CCNP, CCSP, CCVP, Cisco, the Cisco Certified Internetwork Expert logo, Cisco IOS, Cisco Press, Cisco Systems, Cisco Systems Capital, the Cisco Systems logo, Cisco Unity, Collaboration Without Limitation, EtherFast, EtherSwitch, Event Center, Fast Step, Follow Me Browsing, FormShare, GigaDrive, HomeLink, Internet Quotient, IOS, iPhone, iQuick Study, IronPort, the IronPort logo, LightStream, Linksys, MediaTone, MeetingPlace, MeetingPlace Chime Sound, MGX, Networkers, Networking Academy, Network Registrar, PCNow, PIX, PowerPanels, ProConnect, ScriptShare, SenderBase, SMARTnet, Spectrum Expert, StackWise, The Fastest Way to Increase Your Internet Quotient, TransPath, WebEx, and the WebEx logo are registered trademarks of Cisco Systems, Inc. and/or its affiliates in the United States and certain other countries.

All other trademarks mentioned in this document or website are the property of their respective owners. The use of the word partner does not imply a partnership relationship between Cisco and any other company. (0812R)

Contents at a Glance

Contents

Command Syntax Conventions

The conventions used to present command syntax in this book are the same conventions used in the IOS Command Reference. The Command Reference describes these conventions as follows:

- **Boldface** indicates commands and keywords that are entered literally as shown. In actual configuration examples and output (not general command syntax), boldface indicates commands that are manually input by the user (such as a **show** command).

- *Italic* indicates arguments for which you supply actual values.

- Vertical bars (|) separate alternative, mutually exclusive elements.

- Square brackets ([ ]) indicate an optional element.

- Braces ({ }) indicate a required choice.

- Braces within brackets ([{ }]) indicate a required choice within an optional element.

About This Course Booklet

Your Cisco Networking Academy Course Booklet is designed as a study resource you can easily read, highlight, and review on the go, wherever the Internet is not available or practical:

- The text is extracted directly, word-for-word, from the online course so you can highlight important points and take notes in the "Your Chapter Notes" section.

- Headings with the exact page correlations provide a quick reference to the online course for your classroom discussions and exam preparation.

- An icon system directs you to the online curriculum to take full advantage of the images, labs, Packet Tracer activities, and dynamic Flash-based activities embedded within the Networking Academy online course interface.

The Course Booklet is a faster, economical paper-based way to help you succeed with the Cisco Networking Academy online course.

Welcome

Welcome to the CCNA Discovery course, Networking for Home and Small Businesses. The goal of this course is to introduce you to fundamental networking concepts and technologies. This course provides a hands-on introduction to networking and the Internet using tools and hardware commonly found in the home and small business environment. These online materials will assist you in developing the skills necessary to plan and implement small networks across a range of applications. This course prepares you with the skills needed to obtain entry-level Home Network Installer jobs. It also prepares you for some of the skills needed for Network Technician, Computer Technician, Cable Installer, and Help Desk Technician jobs.

More than just information

This computer-based learning environment is an important part of the overall course experience for students and instructors in the Networking Academy. These online course materials are designed to be used along with several other instructional tools and activities. These include:

- Class presentation, discussion, and practice with your instructor
- Hands-on labs that use networking equipment within the Networking Academy classroom
- Online scored assessments and grade book
- Packet Tracer 4.1 simulation tool
- Additional software for classroom activities

A global community

When you participate in the Networking Academy, you are joining a global community linked by common goals and technologies. Schools, colleges, universities and other entities in over 160 countries participate in the program. You can see an interactive network map of the global Networking Academy community at http://www.academynetspace.com.

The material in this course encompasses a broad range of technologies that facilitate how people work, live, play, and learn by communicating with voice, video, and other data. Networking and the Internet affect people differently in different parts of the world. Although we have worked with instructors from around the world to create these materials, it is important that you work with your instructor and fellow students to make the material in this course applicable to your local situation.

Keep in Touch

These online instructional materials, as well as the rest of the course tools, are part of the larger Networking Academy. The portal for the program is located at http://cisco.netacad.net. There you will obtain access to the other tools in the program such as the assessment server and student grade book), as well as informational updates and other relevant links.

Mind Wide Open®

An important goal in education is to enrich you, the student, by expanding what you know and can do. It is important to realize, however, that the instructional materials and the instructor can only facilitate the process. You must make the commitment yourself to learn new skills. Below are a few suggestions to help you learn and grow.

1. Take notes. Professionals in the networking field often keep Engineering Journals in which they write down the things they observe and learn. Taking notes is an important way to help your understanding grow over time.

2. Think about it. The course provides information both to change what you know and what you can do. As you go through the course, ask yourself what makes sense and what doesn't. Stop and ask questions when you are confused. Try to find out more about topics that interest you. If you are not sure why something is being taught, consider asking your instructor or a friend. Think about how the different parts of the course fit together.

3. Practice. Learning new skills requires practice. We believe this is so important to e-learning that we have a special name for it. We call it e-doing. It is very important that you complete the activities in the online instructional materials and that you also complete the hands-on labs and Packet Tracer® activities.

4. Practice again. Have you ever thought that you knew how to do something and then, when it was time to show it on a test or at work, you discovered that you really hadn't mastered it? Just like learning any new skill like a sport, game, or language, learning a professional skill requires patience and repeated practice before you can say you have truly learned it. The online instructional materials in this course provide opportunities for repeated practice for many skills. Take full advantage of them. You can also work with your instructor to extend Packet Tracer, and other tools, for additional practice as needed.

5. Teach it. Teaching a friend or colleague is often a good way to reinforce your own learning. To teach well, you will have to work through details that you may have overlooked on your first reading. Conversations about the course material with fellow students, colleagues, and the instructor can help solidify your understanding of networking concepts.

6. Make changes as you go. The course is designed to provide feedback through interactive activities and quizzes, the online assessment system, and through interactions with your instructor. You can use this feedback to better understand where your strengths and weaknesses are. If there is an area that you are having trouble with, focus on studying or practicing more in that area. Seek additional feedback from your instructor and other students.

Explore the world of networking

This version of the course includes a special tool called Packet Tracer 4.1®. Packet Tracer is a networking learning tool that supports a wide range of physical and logical simulations. It also provides visualization tools to help you to understand the internal workings of a network.

The Packet Tracer activities included in the course consist of network simulations, games, activities, and challenges that provide a broad range of learning experiences.

Create your own worlds

You can also use Packet Tracer to create your own experiments and networking scenarios. We hope that, over time, you consider using Packet Tracer – not only for experiencing the activities included in the course, but also to become an author, explorer, and experimenter.

The online course materials have embedded Packet Tracer activities that will launch on computers running Windows® operating systems, if Packet Tracer is installed. This integration may also work on other operating systems using Windows emulation.

CHAPTER 1

Personal Computer Hardware

Introduction

Refer to
Figure
in online course

1.1 Personal Computers and Applications

Refer to
Figure
in online course

1.1.1 How and Where Computers are Used

Computers play an increasingly important and nearly indispensable role in everyday life.

Computers are used all over the world and in all types of environments. They are used in businesses, manufacturing environments, homes, government offices and non-profit organizations. Schools use computers for instruction and for maintaining student records. Hospitals use computers to maintain patient records and to provide medical care.

In addition to these types of computers, there are also many customized computers designed for specific purposes. These computers can be integrated into devices such as televisions, cash registers, sound systems, and other electronic devices. They can even be found embedded in appliances such as stoves and refrigerators and used in automobiles, and aircraft.

Where are computers found within your environment?

Refer to
Figure
in online course

Computers are used for many reasons and in many different places. They may be of different sizes and processing power, but all computers have some features in common. In order for most computers to perform useful functions, there are three things that have to work together:

Step 1.   Hardware - the physical components, both internal and external, that make up a computer.

Step 2.   Operating System - a set of computer programs that manages the *hardware* of a computer. An operating system controls the resources on a computer, including *memory* and *disk storage*. An example of an operating system is *Windows XP*.

Step 3.   Application Software - programs loaded on the computer to perform a specific function using the capabilities of the computer. An example of *application* software is a word processor or a computer game.

1.1.2 Local and Network Applications

Refer to
Figure
in online course

The *computer* is only as useful as the program or application on it. Applications can be divided into two general categories:

Business/Industry Software - Software designed for use by a specific industry or market. Examples include: medical practice management tools, educational tools and legal software.

General Use Software - Software used by a wide range of organizations and home users for various purposes. These applications can be used by any business or individual.

General use software includes integrated applications packages known as Office Suites. They usually include applications such as word processing, *spreadsheet*, *database*, presentation and email/contacts/schedule management.

Other popular applications include graphics editing software and multimedia authoring applications. These tools allow users to manipulate photos as well as create rich media presentations that use voice, video and graphics.

Refer to
Figure
in online course

In addition to Business/Industry and General Use software, an application can be classified as local or networked.

Local application - A *local application* is a program, such as a word processor, that is stored on the *hard disk* of the computer. The application runs only on that computer.

Network application - A *network application* is one that is designed to run over a network, such as the *Internet*. A network application has two components, one that runs on the local computer and one that runs on a remote computer. Email is an example of a network application.

Most computers have a combination of local and network applications installed.

Refer to
Interactive Graphic
in online course.

Activity

Classify applications based on a given scenario.

Check the appropriate boxes to classify the application as business/industry or general and local or networked.

1.2 Types of Computers

1.2.1 Classes of Computers

Refer to
Figure
in online course

There are many different types of computers available including:

- Mainframes
- Servers
- Desktops
- Workstations
- Laptops
- Hand-held portable devices

Each type of computer has been designed with a particular purpose in mind, such as portable access to information, processing of detailed graphics, and so on.

The most common types of computers used in homes and businesses are servers, workstations, desktops, laptops and other portable devices. Mainframes, on the other hand, are large centralized computers found in sizeable enterprises and purchased through specialized resellers.

1.2.2 Servers, Desktops and Workstations

Refer to
Figure
in online course

Servers

Servers are high performance computers used in businesses and other organizations. Servers provide services to many end users or clients.

Server hardware is optimized for quick response time to multiple *network* requests. Servers have multiple Central Processing Units (CPUs), large amounts of Random Access Memory (*RAM*) and multiple high capacity disk drives that provide very fast information retrieval.

The services provided by a *server* are often important and may need to be available to users at all times. Servers, therefore, often contain duplicate, or redundant, parts to prevent them from failing. Automatic and manual *backup* of data is also usually done on a regular basis. Servers are usually kept in secure areas where access is controlled.

Their design may be one of several types: they can be a standalone tower design, be rack mounted, or have a *blade* design. Since a server is typically used as a storage point and not a day-to-day end-user device, it may not have a monitor or keyboard, or may share a monitor and keyboard with other devices.

Common services found on a server include file storage, *email* storage, web pages, print sharing and others.

Refer to
Figure
in online course

Desktops

Desktops support many options and capabilities. A wide variety of cases, power supplies, hard drives, video cards, monitors and other components are available. Desktops can have many different connection types, video options, and a wide array of supported peripherals.

Desktops are commonly used to run applications such as word processing, spreadsheets and networked applications such as email and web browsing.

There is another type of computer that may look similar to a desktop, but is much more powerful: the workstation.

Refer to
Figure
in online course

Workstation

Workstations are high-powered business computers. They are designed for specialized, high-end applications like engineering programs such as *CAD* (Computer Aided Design). Workstations are used in 3-D graphics design, video animation and virtual reality simulation. They may also be used as management stations for telecommunications or medical equipment. As with servers, workstations typically have multiple CPUs, large amounts of RAM and multiple, high-capacity disk drives that are very fast. Workstations usually have very powerful graphics capabilities and a large monitor or multiple monitors.

Servers, desktops and workstations are all designed as stationary devices. They are not portable, like laptops.

Refer to
Interactive Graphic
in online course.

Activity

Determine the type of computer to use based on a given scenario.

Check the appropriate answer for each scenario.

1.2.3 Portable Devices

Refer to
Figure
in online course

In addition to various types of stationary computers, there are many portable electronic devices available.

These portable devices vary in size, power and graphic capability and include:

- Laptop or notebook PC
- Tablet PC
- Pocket PC
- Personal Digital Assistant (*PDA*)
- Gaming device
- Cell phones

Laptops, also called notebooks, are comparable to desktops in usage and processing capability. However, they are portable devices built to be lightweight and use less power, with a built-in mouse, monitor and keyboard. Laptops can also be plugged into a *docking station* which allows the user to utilize a larger monitor, mouse, full-sized keyboard and have more connection options.

Despite this, laptops have a limited number of configurations available, such as video options and connection types. They are also not as easily upgradeable as the desktop.

Refer to
Figure
in online course

Other portable devices, such as PDAs or pocket PCs, have less powerful CPUs and less RAM. They have small screens with limited display capabilities and may have a small input keyboard.

The key advantage of portable computers is that information and services are available immediately, almost anywhere. For example, mobile phones have built-in address books for contact names and telephone numbers. PDAs are available with built-in telephone, web *browser*, email, and other software.

The functions of these individual devices can be combined into one multifunction device. The multifunction device can combine a PDA, *cell phone*, *digital* camera, and music player. It can provide Internet access and wireless networking capability, but has limited processing power similar to the PDA.

1.3 Binary Representation of Data

1.3.1 Representing Information Digitally

Refer to
Figure
in online course

Within a computer, information is represented and stored in a digital *binary* format. The term *bit* is an abbreviation of *binary digit* and represents the smallest piece of data. Humans interpret words and pictures; computers interpret only patterns of bits.

A bit can have only two possible values, a one digit (1) or a zero digit (0). A bit can be used to represent the state of something that has two states. For example, a light switch can be either On or Off; in binary representation, these states would correspond to 1 and 0 respectively.

Computers use binary codes to represent and interpret letters, numbers and special characters with bits. A commonly used code is the American Standard Code for Information Interchange (*ASCII*). With ASCII, each character is represented by a string of bits. For example:

Capital letter: **A** = 01000001

Number: **9** = 00111001

Special character: # = 00100011

Each group of eight bits, such as the representations of letters and numbers, is known as a *byte*.

Codes can be used to represent almost any type of information digitally: computer data, graphics, photos, voice, video and music.

1.3.2 Measuring Data Storage Capacity

Refer to
Figure
in online course

While a bit is the smallest representation of data, the most basic unit of digital storage is the byte. A byte is 8 bits and is the smallest unit of measure (*UOM*) used to represent data storage capacity.

When referring to storage space, we use the terms bytes (B), kilobytes (KB), megabytes (MB), gigabytes (*GB*), and terabytes (*TB*).

One kilobyte is a little more than one thousand bytes, specifically 1,024. A megabyte represents more than a million bytes or 1,048,576. A gigabyte is 1,073,741,824 bytes and so on. The exact number is gained by taking 2^n power. Example: KB = 2^{10}; MB = 2^{20}; GB = 2^{30}.

In general, when something is represented digitally, the greater the detail, the greater the number of bits needed to represent it. A low-resolution picture from a digital camera will use around 360KB, and a high-resolution picture could use 2 MB or more.

Kilobytes, megabytes, gigabytes, and terabytes are typically used to measure the size or storage capacity of a device. Examples of components and devices that use byte storage include: random access memory (RAM), hard disk drive space, CDs, DVDs, and MP3 players.

Refer to
Lab Activity
for this chapter

Lab Activity

Determine the size of the hard disk and the amount of RAM installed on your computer.

1.3.3 Measuring Speed, Resolution and Frequency

Refer to
Figure
in online course

Refer to
Figure
in online course

One of the advantages of digital information is that it can be transmitted over long distances without the quality becoming degraded. A *modem* is used to convert the binary information into a form suitable for transmitting through the medium.

Commonly used media are:

- Cables, which use pulses of electricity through copper wires

- Fiber optics, which use pulses of light over fibers made from glass or plastic

- Wireless, which uses pulses of low-power radio waves

Refer to
Figure
in online course

There are two measures for the size of a file: bits (b) and bytes (B). Communication engineers think in terms of transferring bits, whereas computer users think in terms of file sizes, which are usually measured in Bytes (such as kilobytes, megabytes, etc). There are eight bits to one byte.

The data rate determines how long it will take to transfer a file. The larger the file, the longer it takes, because there is more information to transfer. Data transfer rates are measured in thousands of bits per second (*kbps*) or millions of bits per second (Mbps). Notice, that in the kbps abbreviation, a lower case k is used instead of the upper case K. This is because when talking about the transfer of data, most engineers round the number down. So a kbps actually refers to the transfer of 1000 bits of information in one second, whereas a Kbps would refer to the transfer of 1024 bits of information in one second. A *DSL* or a *cable modem* can operate in ranges of 512 kbps, 2 Mbps or higher depending on the technology being used.

Download time

Calculated download times are theoretical and depend on cable connection, computer processor speed and other overheads. To get an estimate of the length of time it takes to download a file, divide the file size by the data rate. For example, how long will it take to transfer a low resolution digital photo of 256KB via a 512kbps cable connection? First step, convert the file size into bits: 8 x 256 x 1024 = 2097152 bits. 256KB corresponds to 2097 kb. Notice that the 2097152 is rounded to the nearest 1000, so lower case k is used. The download time is then 2097 kb divided by 512 kbps, which equates to approximately 4 seconds.

Refer to **Figure** in online course

In addition to storage capacity and data transfer speed, there are other units of measure when working with computers.

Computer Screen Resolution

Graphics resolution is measured in pixels. A pixel is a distinct point of light displayed on a monitor. The quality of a computer screen is defined by the number of horizontal and vertical pixels that can be displayed. For example a widescreen monitor may be able to display 1280 x 1024 pixels with millions of colors. As for image resolution in digital cameras, it is measured by the number of mega pixels that can captured in a photograph.

Analog Frequencies

Hertz is a measurement of how fast something cycles or refreshes. One hertz represents one cycle per second. In computers, the speed of the computer processor is measured by how fast it can cycle in order to execute instructions, measured in hertz. For example, a processor that runs at 300 *MHz* (megahertz) executes 300 million cycles per second. Wireless transmissions and radio frequencies are also measured in hertz.

Refer to **Lab Activity** for this chapter

Lab Activity

Determine the screen resolution of your computer.

1.4 Computer Components and Peripherals

1.4.1 Computer System

Refer to **Figure** in online course

There are many types of computers. What makes one computer better suited to play a new game or play a new audio file over another? The answer is the components and peripherals that make up the computer system.

The requirements for a machine dedicated mainly to word processing are very different than one designed for graphics applications or gaming. It is important to determine the intended uses for a computer before deciding on the type of computer and components to purchase.

Many manufacturers mass produce computer systems and sell them either through direct marketing or retail chains. These computer systems are designed to function well for a variety of tasks. There are also a number of vendors that can custom assemble computer systems to the end-user's specifications. There are advantages and disadvantages for both.

Refer to **Figure** in online course

Preassembled Computer

Advantages:

- Lower cost

- Adequate to perform most applications

- No waiting period for assembly

- Typically used by less knowledgeable consumers who do not require special needs

Disadvantages:

- Often lack the performance level that can be obtained from custom built computers

Custom Built Computer

Advantages:

- The end-user can specify exact components that meet user needs

- Generally support higher performance applications such as graphics, gaming, and server applications

Disadvantages:

- Generally more costly than a preassembled device

- Longer waiting periods for assembly

It is also possible to purchase the individual parts and component of a computer and build it. Regardless of the decision to buy a preassembled or custom built system or build it, the final product must match the requirements of the end user. Some of the items to consider when purchasing a computer include: the *motherboard*, processor, RAM, storage, adapter cards, as well as the case and power options.

1.4.2 Motherboard, CPU, and RAM

Refer to
Figure
in online course

A motherboard is a large *circuit* board used to connect the electronics and circuitry required which comprise the computer system. Motherboards contain connectors which allow major system components such as the *CPU* and RAM to attach to the board. The motherboard moves data between the various connections and system components.

A motherboard can also contain connector slots for network, video and sound cards. However, many motherboards now come equipped with these features as integrated components. The difference between the two is how they are upgraded. When using connectors on the motherboard, system components are easily unplugged and changed or upgraded as technology advances.

When upgrading or replacing an on-board feature, it cannot be removed from the motherboard. Therefore, it is often necessary to disable the on-board functionality and add an additional dedicated card using a connector.

When selecting a motherboard it must:

- Support the selected CPU type and speed

- Support the amount and type of system RAM required by the applications

- Have sufficient slots of the correct type to accept all required *interface* cards

- Have sufficient interfaces of the correct type

Refer to
Figure
in online course

Central Processing Unit (CPU)

The CPU, or processor, is the nerve center of the computer system. It is the component that processes all of the data within the machine. The type of CPU should be the first decision made when building or updating a computer system. Important factors when selecting a CPU are the processor speed and bus speed.

Processor Speed

Processor speed measures how fast a CPU cycles information. It is generally measured in MHz or *GHz*. The higher the speed the faster the performance. Faster processors consume more power and create more heat than their slower counterparts. For this reason, mobile devices, such as *laptop* computers, typically use processors that are slower and consume less power in order to extend the time they can operate using batteries.

Bus Speed

CPUs transfer data between various types of memory on the system board during its operation. The pathway for this movement of data is called the bus. In general, the faster the bus, the faster the computer will be.

When selecting a CPU, keep in mind that applications continue to evolve. Purchasing a CPU of moderate speed may satisfy current requirements. Future applications, however, may be more complicated and require, for example, fast high resolution graphics; if the CPU is not sufficiently fast, the overall performance, measured in terms of response time, will be slower.

The CPU is mounted through a socket on the motherboard and is normally the largest component on the board. The motherboard must be equipped with a compatible socket to accept the selected CPU.

Refer to
Figure
in online course

RAM is a type of data storage used in computers. It is used to store programs and data while being processed by the CPU. Stored data is accessed in any order, or at random, as needed. All computer programs run from RAM. Besides the CPU, the amount of RAM is the most important factor in computer performance.

Every operating system requires a minimal amount of RAM in order for the *OS* to function. Most computers are capable of running multiple applications simultaneously, or multi-tasking. For example, many users run email programs, Instant Messenger clients, as well as anti-virus tools or *firewall* software. All of these applications require memory. The more applications that need to run simultaneously, the more RAM required.

More RAM is also recommended for computer systems with multiple processors. Additionally, as the speed of the CPU and the bus increase, so must the speed of the memory it accesses. The amount and type of RAM that can be installed on a system is dictated by the motherboard.

1.4.3 Adapter Cards

Refer to
Figure
in online course

Adapter cards add functionality to a computer system. They are designed to be plugged into a connector or slot on the motherboard and become part of the system. Many motherboards are designed to incorporate the functionality of these adapter cards on the motherboard itself thus removing the necessity to purchase and install separate cards. While this does provide basic functionality, the addition of dedicated adapter cards can often provide an enhanced level of performance.

Some of the more common adapter cards include:

- Video cards

- Sound cards

- Network interface cards

- Modems

- Interface cards

- Controller cards

1.4.4 Storage Devices

Refer to **Figure** in online course

When power is removed from the computer, any data stored in RAM is lost. Programs and user data must be stored in a form that will not disappear when the power is removed. This is known as non-volatile storage. Many types of non-volatile storage are available for computer systems including:

- Read only: *CD*, *DVD*
- Write once: *CD-R*, *DVD-R*
- Write many: *CD-RW*, *DVD-RW*

Magnetic Storage

Magnetic storage devices are the most common form found in computers. These devices store information in the form of magnetic fields. They include:

- Hard disk drives
- Floppy drives
- Tape drives

Refer to **Figure** in online course

Optical Drives

Optical storage devices use *laser* beams to record information by creating differences in optical density. These devices include CDs and DVDs and come in three different formats:

- Read only: CD, DVD
- Write once: CD-R, DVD-R
- Write many: CD-RW, DVD-RW

The prices of these devices continue to fall and most computers now incorporate DVD-RW drives that can store approximately 4.7 GB of data on a single disc.

Another form of DVD drive, called Blu-ray is also available. It uses a different type of laser to read and write data. The color of the laser used to store this information is blue-violet. For this reason, disks are called Blu-ray, to distinguish them from conventional DVDs which use a red laser. Blu-ray disks have storage capacities of 25 GB and more.

Static Memory and Memory Sticks

Static memory devices use memory chips to store information. This information is retained even after power is turned off. They connect to a *USB* port on the computer and offer capacities of 128 MB or more. Due to their size and shape, these devices are known as USB memory keys or flash drives and have widely replaced floppy disks for transportation of files between systems. Many portable and hand-held devices rely entirely on static memory for storage.

When purchasing storage for a computer system, it is generally good practice to have a mix of magnetic storage, optical drives as well as static memory available. When determining storage requirements, be sure to allow for growth by adding an additional 20% of storage above estimated needs.

1.4.5 Peripheral Devices

Refer to **Figure** in online course

A peripheral is a device that is added to the computer to expand its capabilities. These devices are optional in nature and are not required for the basic functioning of the computer. Instead they are used to increase the usefulness of the machine. Peripheral devices are connected externally to the computer using a specialized cable or wireless connection.

Peripheral devices can fit into one of four categories: input, output, storage or networking devices. Examples of some common peripherals include:

- *Input devices* - trackball, joystick, scanner, digital camera, digitizer, barcode reader, microphone
- *Output devices* - *printer*, plotter, speakers, headphones
- *Storage devices* - secondary hard drive, external CD/DVD devices, flash drives
- *Networking* - external modems, external *NIC*

1.4.6 Cases and Power Supplies

Case and Power Supply

Once all internal components and connections are determined, the case is the next consideration. Some cases are designed to sit on top of the user's desk while others sit below the desk. Computers designed to sit on the desk provide easy access to interfaces and drives but occupy valuable desk space. A tower or mini-tower can either be used on the desk or sit beneath the table. Whatever the case style, select one that has enough space for all components.

The case and *power supply* are usually sold together as a unit. The power supply must be sufficient to power the system and any devices that are added to it in the future.

Computer systems require a steady supply of continuous power. The power from many electricity supply companies is subject to voltage reductions and cuts. A poor supply can affect the performance of computer hardware and possibly damage it. These power issues can also corrupt software and data.

In order to help protect the computer system from these power problems, devices such as surge suppressors and uninterruptible power supplies (*UPS*) have been developed.

Surge Suppressor

A surge suppressor is designed to remove voltage spikes and surges from the power line and prevent them from damaging a computer system. They are relatively inexpensive and easy to install.

Generally the surge suppressor is plugged into the power outlet and the computer system is plugged into the surge suppressor. Many surge suppressors also have connectors for phone lines to protect modems from damage due to voltage surges that may be carried through the telephone lines.

Uninterruptible Power Supplies

A UPS is a device that continually monitors the power to a computer system and maintains the charge on an internal battery. If the power is interrupted, the UPS provides backup power to the system without interruption. The backup power comes from a battery inside the UPS and can only power the computer system for a short period of time. UPSs are designed to provide the end-user with sufficient time to properly shut down a computer system should the main power fail. A UPS can also provide an even flow of power to the computer and prevent damage caused by voltage surges.

UPSs suitable for home and small business use are relatively inexpensive and often incorporate surge suppressors and other functionality to stabilize the power supplied by the utilities company. It is highly recommended that all computers be protected by a UPS regardless of their functionality or location.

1.5 Computer System Components

1.5.1 Safety and Best Practices

Refer to
Figure
in online course

Computers are a collection of very complex components and peripherals, all working together to accomplish a task. Occasionally one of these components fails, or needs to be upgraded to improve the functionality of the system. This may require opening the computer and working inside the case.

When working inside a computer case, it is important to keep precautions in mind to prevent damage to the system components as well as harm to the technician. Before the computer case is opened, make sure the computer is switched off and the power cable is unplugged.

Computer systems and monitors can be very heavy and should be lifted with caution. Before opening a computer system be sure to have a proper work area. The work area should be a clean flat surface, strong enough to support the weight of heavy equipment. It should be well organized, free from clutter and distractions, and adequately lit to prevent eye stain.

Wear proper eye protection to prevent accumulated dust, small screws, and components from causing damage to the eyes. Additionally, when opening a computer case, be aware there are sharp edges that should be avoided.

Power supplies and monitors operate at dangerously high voltages and should only be opened by individuals with special training.

Refer to
Figure
in online course

Some computer systems are specially designed to enable components to be hot-swapped, meaning that it is not necessary to turn off the computer before adding or removing components. This feature allows the system to remain operational during repairs or upgrades and is usually found in high performance servers.

Unless you are sure that the system is *hot-swappable*, turn it off before opening the case or removing components. Inserting or removing components with the power on, in a system that is not hot-swappable, can cause permanent and serious damage to the system and technician.

Internal system components are especially sensitive to static electricity. *ESD* (Electrostatic Discharge) is static electricity that can be transferred from your body to electronic components in the computer. The static electricity doesn't have to be felt by you in order to occur.

ESD can cause catastrophic failures in components, making them non-functional. ESD can also cause intermittent faults which are very difficult to isolate. For this reason, proper grounding is essential. A special wrist grounding strap is used to connect the technician to the computer case. Grounding ensures that they both reach the same voltage potential and ESD is prevented.

Refer to
Figure
in online course

Excess force should never be used when installing components. Excessive force can damage both the motherboard and the component being installed, and can prevent the system from functioning properly. Damage is not always visible. Force can also damage connectors which, in turn, can damage new system components.

In order to make certain that all safety precautions are followed it is a good idea to create a safety checklist which can be followed.

1.5.2 Installing Components and Verifying Operation

Refer to
Figure
in online course

The following procedures apply to most system components.

Step 1.   Determine if the computer component is hot-swappable. If not, or if in doubt, unplug the system unit before opening the case.

Step 2.   Attach a grounding strap from your body to the system framework, or chassis, to prevent any damage which may be caused by ESD.

Step 3.   If replacing a component, remove the old component. Components are often held into the system with small screws or clips. When removing screws do not to let them drop on the system motherboard. Also, be careful not to break any plastic clips.

Step 4.   Check the connection type on the new component. Each card is designed to work only with a certain type of connector and should not be forced when inserting or removing the card.

Step 5.   Place the new component in the correct connection slot, with the correct orientation, carefully following all installation instructions that may have accompanied the component.

Follow safety precautions throughout the process.

Refer to
Figure
in online course

Once the component has been added or upgraded, close the case and reconnect the power and other cables. Switch on the system and watch for any messages that may appear on the screen. If the system fails to start, disconnect all cables and verify that the component was properly installed. If the system still will not start with the new component installed, remove it and try to start the system. If the system starts without the new component, the component may not be compatible with the current hardware and software and additional research into the problem is required.

Certain components require the addition of a specialized piece of software, or *driver*, to function. For commonly encountered components the drivers are usually contained in the operating system itself but for more specialized components the driver must be added separately. Newer operating systems will usually prompt for the addition of any required drivers.

Drivers are continually updated to improve efficiency and functionality. The most current driver can be obtained from the manufacturer's web site and should normally be used. Always read any documentation that accompanies the driver software for potential problems and the proper installation procedure.

Refer to
Figure
in online course

Once installed, the component should be tested for complete functionality.

Components are designed to make use of specific sets of *system resources*. If two components try to use the same resources one, or both, will fail. The solution is to change the resources used by one of the devices. Newer components and operating systems are able to dynamically assign system resources.

If the device fails to function properly, verify that the correct and most recent driver is installed. Also check that the operating system has correctly detected and identified the device. If this fails to correct the problem, power down the system, carefully reseat the component, and verify that all connections are correct. Check the component documentation for the correct settings. If the device continues to be non-functional, it is possible that the component is defective and it should be returned to the vendor.

1.5.3 Installing Peripherals and Verifying Operation

Refer to
Figure
in online course

Peripheral devices, unlike internal components, do not require the computer case to be opened for installation. Peripherals connect to an interface on the outside of the case with a wired or wireless link. Historically peripherals were designed to function when connected to a specific type of port. For example, Personal Computer printers were designed to connect to a parallel port which transferred data from the computer to the printer in a specific format.

More recently the development of the Universal Serial Bus (USB) interface has greatly simplified the connection of peripheral devices that use wires. USB devices require no complex configurations and can merely be plugged into an appropriate interface assuming the proper driver has been installed. There have also been an increasing number of peripheral devices which connect to the *host* computer through wireless technology.

Refer to
Figure
in online course

The installation of a *peripheral device* requires several steps. The order and detail of these steps varies depending on the type of physical connection and whether or not the peripheral is a Plug-and-Play (*PnP*) device. The steps include:

- Connect the peripheral to the host using the appropriate cable or wireless connection
- Connect the peripheral to a power source
- Install the appropriate driver

Some old peripheral devices, so-called legacy devices, are not PnP enabled. For these, driver installation occurs after the device has been connected to the computer and powered up.

For PnP enabled USB devices, the driver is preinstalled on the system. In this case, when the PnP device is connected and powered on, the operating system recognizes the device and installs the appropriate driver.

Installation of outdated or wrong drivers can cause a peripheral device to behave unpredictably. For this reason, it is necessary to install the most current drivers available.

Refer to
Figure
in online course

If the peripheral device does not function once connected and installed, verify that all cables have been properly connected and that the device is powered up.

Many devices, such as printers, offer a testing functionality on the device directly, and not through the computer. Use this feature to verify that the device itself is functioning properly. If the device is operational, but not connecting to the computer system, the problem could be with the cable connection.

Swap the suspect cable with a known good one. If this fails to solve the problem the next step is to verify that the connection port the peripheral device is connected to is recognized by the operating system.

If everything appears to be functioning properly the device may not be compatible with the current hardware or operating system and requires more research to solve the problem.

Once installed, the full functionality of the peripheral device must be tested. If only partial functionality is available the most likely cause is an outdated driver. This is easily remedied by downloading and installing the most current driver from the manufacturer's web site.

Refer to
Lab Activity
for this chapter

Lab Activity

Install a directly connected printer and verify operation.

Summary

Quiz

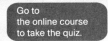

Take the chapter quiz to check your knowledge.

Your Chapter Notes

CHAPTER 2

Operating Systems

Introduction

Refer to **Figure** in online course

2.1 Choosing the Operating Systems

2.1.1 Purpose of an Operating System

Refer to **Figure** in online course

System components and peripherals, by themselves, are nothing more than a collection of electronics and mechanical parts. To get these parts to work together to perform a specific task, a special type of computer program, known as an operating system (OS), is required.

Suppose that a user wants to write a report and print it out on an attached printer. A word processing application is required to accomplish this task. Information is entered from the keyboard, displayed on the monitor, saved on the disk drive and then finally sent to the printer.

In order for the word processing program to accomplish all of this, it must work with the OS, which controls input and output functions. In addition, the entered data is manipulated inside of the computer, stored in RAM and processed by the CPU. This internal manipulation and processing is also controlled by the OS. All computerized devices, such as servers, desktops, laptops or handhelds, require an OS in order to function.

Refer to **Figure** in online course

The OS acts like a translator between user applications and the hardware. A user interacts with the computer system through an application, such as a word processor, spreadsheet, computer game or *instant messaging* program. Application programs are designed for a specific purpose, such as word processing, and know nothing of the underlying electronics. For example, the application is not concerned with how information is entered into the application from the keyboard. The operating system is responsible for the communication between the application and the hardware.

When a computer is powered on, it loads the OS, normally from a disk drive, into RAM. The portion of the OS code that interacts directly with the computer hardware is known as the *kernel*. The portion that interfaces with the applications and user, is known as the *shell*. The user can interact with the shell using either the command line interface (*CLI*) or graphical user interface (*GUI*).

When using the CLI, the user interacts directly with the system in a text-based environment by entering commands on the keyboard at a command prompt. The system executes the command, often providing textual output. The GUI interface allows the user to interact with the system in an environment that uses graphical images, multimedia, and text. Actions are performed by interacting with the images on screen. GUI is more user friendly and requires less knowledge than CLI of the command structure to utilize the system. For this reason, many individuals rely on the GUI environments. Most operating systems offer both GUI and CLI.

Refer to **Figure** in online course

Operating systems have complete control of local hardware resources. They are designed to work with one user at a time. They enable the user to multitask. The operating system keeps track of which resources are used by which application.

In order to work with resources that are not directly connected to the computer system, a special piece of software must be added that allows a device to send and receive data from the network. This software, known as a *redirector*, may either be an integral part of the OS or may need to be installed separately as a *network client*. When installed, the operating system becomes a network operating system (*NOS*).

A NOS offers complex scheduling and user management software that allow a device to share resources between many users and treat networked resources as though they are directly connected.

2.1.2 Operating System Requirements

Refer to **Figure** in online course

There are many different operating systems available. The major groupings are listed here with some examples.

- Microsoft Windows: XP, Vista, 2003 Server
- UNIX-Based: IBM *AIX*, Hewlett Packard HPUX, and Sun Solaris
- BSD - Free BSD
- Linux-Based (Many varieties)
- Macintosh OS X
- Non-Unix Proprietary: IBM *OS/400*, *z/OS*

While most of these operating systems require the user to purchase and agree to a commercial license, there are several operating systems released under a different type of licensing scheme known as the *GNU* Public License (*GPL*).

Commercial licenses usually deny end-users the ability to modify the program in any way. Windows XP, Mac OS X and UNIX are all examples of commercial OS software.

In contrast, the GPL allows end-users to modify and enhance the code, if they desire, to better suit their environment. Some common operating systems, which are released under the GPL, include Linux and BSD.

Refer to **Figure** in online course

Operating systems require a certain amount of hardware resources. These resources are specified by the manufacturer and include such things as:

- Amount of RAM
- Hard disk space required
- Processor type and speed
- Video resolution

Manufacturers often specify both a minimum and recommended level of hardware resources. System performance at the minimum specified hardware configuration is usually poor and only sufficient to support the OS and no other functionality. The recommended configuration is usually the better option and is more likely to support standard additional applications and resources.

To take advantage of all of the features provided by an operating system, additional hardware resources such as sound cards, NICs, modems, microphones, and speakers are generally required. Many of the OS developers test various hardware devices and certify that they are compatible with the operating system. Always confirm that the hardware has been certified to work with the operating system before purchasing and installing it.

Refer to
Figure
in online course

Refer to
Figure
in online course

2.1.3 Operating System Selection

Choosing an appropriate OS requires many factors to be considered before deciding which one to use in a given environment.

The first step in selecting an OS is to ensure that the OS being considered fully supports the requirements of the end user. Does the OS support the applications that will be run? Is the security and functionality sufficient for the needs of the users?

Next, conduct research to make sure that sufficient hardware resources are available to support the OS. This includes such basic items as memory, processors, and disk space, as well as peripheral devices such as scanners, sound cards, NICs and removable storage.

Another consideration is the level of human resources needed to support the OS. In a business environment, a company may limit support to one or two operating systems and discourage, or even disallow, the installation of any other OS. In the home environment, the ready availability of technical support for an OS may be a determining factor.

Refer to
Figure
in online course

When considering implementing an OS, it is the total cost of ownership (*TCO*) of the OS that must be considered in the decision making process. This not only includes the costs of obtaining and installing the OS, but also all costs associated with supporting it.

Another factor that may come into play in the decision making process is the availability of the operating system. Some countries and/or businesses have made decisions to support a specific type of OS or may have restrictions barring individuals from obtaining certain types of technologies. In this type of environment, it may not be possible to consider a particular OS regardless of its suitability to the task.

The process for selecting an operating system must take all of these factors into account.

2.2 Installing the Operating System

2.2.1 OS Installation Methods

Refer to
Figure
in online course

An OS is installed in a defined section of the hard disk, called a disk *partition*. There are various methods for installing an OS. The method selected for installation is based on the system hardware, the OS being installed, and user requirements. There are four basic options available for the installation of a new OS:

Clean Install

A clean install is done on a new system or in cases where no *upgrade* path exists between the current OS and the one being installed. It deletes all data on the partition where the OS is installed and requires application software to be reinstalled. A new computer system requires a clean install. A clean install is also performed when the existing OS installation has become damaged in some way.

Upgrade

If staying within the same OS platform, it is often possible to do an upgrade. With an upgrade, system configuration settings, applications and data are preserved. It simply replaces the old OS files with the new OS files.

Multi-boot

It is possible to install more than one OS on a computer to create a multi-boot system. Each OS is contained within its own partition and can have its own files and configuration settings. On start-up, the user is presented with a menu to select the desired OS. Only one OS can run at a time and it has full control of the hardware.

Virtualization

Virtualization is a technique that is often deployed on servers. It enables multiple copies of an OS to be run on a single set of hardware, thus creating many virtual machines. Each virtual machine can be treated as a separate computer. This enables a single physical resource to appear to function as multiple logical resources.

Refer to
Figure
in online course

Refer to
Figure
in online course

2.2.2 Preparing for OS Installation

A pre-installation checklist helps ensure that the installation process is successful.

Step 1.   Verify that all hardware is certified to work with the selected OS.

Step 2.   Verify that the hardware resources meet or exceed the published minimum requirements.

Step 3.   Confirm that the appropriate installation medium is available. Due to the file size of current operating systems, they are usually available on both CD and DVD medium.

Step 4.   If the OS is to be installed on a system that already contains data: (a) Use system diagnostic tools and utilities to ensure the current OS installation is in good condition, free of malicious or damaging files and codes; (b) Complete a full backup of all important files.

Step 5.   If performing a clean-install, verify that all application software is available for installation.

Refer to
Figure
in online course

Before starting the installation, it is necessary to determine the partition structure that best meets user requirements.

One of the techniques available to help protect data is to divide the hard drive into multiple partitions. With a clean install, many technicians prefer to create one partition for data and a separate partition for the OS. This enables an OS to be upgraded without the risk of losing data. It also simplifies backup and recovery of data files.

It is also necessary to determine the type of *file system* to use. A file system is the method the OS uses to keep track of the files. Many different file system types exist. Commonly used file systems include *FAT* 16/32, *NTFS*, *HPFS*, *ext2*, *ext3*. Each OS is designed to work with one or more of these file system types and each file system type offers specific advantages. Careful consideration should be made to the type of file systems supported by the selected OS and the benefits of each.

Although tools exist to modify the partitioning structure and file system of a hard drive after installation, these should be avoided if possible. When modifying either the file system or partition structure on a hard drive, *data loss* may result. Careful planning can help preserve the integrity of the data.

2.2.3 Configuring a Computer for the Network

Refer to
Figure
in online course

Once an OS is installed, the computer can be configured to participate in a network. A network is a group of devices, such as computers, that are connected to each other for the purposes of sharing information and resources. Shared resources can include printers, documents and Internet access connections.

To physically connect to a network, a computer must have a network interface card (NIC). The NIC is a piece of hardware that allows a computer to connect to the network medium. It may be integrated into the computer motherboard or may be a separately installed card.

In addition to the physical connection, some configuration of the operating system is required for the computer to participate in the network. Most modern networks connect to the Internet and use the Internet to exchange information. Each computer on these networks requires an Internet Protocol (*IP*) address, as well as other information, to identify it. There are three parts to the IP configuration, which must be correct for the computer to send and receive information on the network. These three parts are:

- *IP address* - identifies the computer on the network.

- **Subnet mask** - is used to identify the network on which the computer is connected.

- **Default gateway** - identifies the device that the computer uses to access the Internet or another network.

Refer to
Figure
in online course

A computer IP address can be configured manually or assigned automatically by another device.

Manual IP Configuration

With manual configuration, the required values are entered into the computer via the keyboard, typically by a network administrator. The IP address entered is referred to as a static address and is permanently assigned to that computer.

Dynamic IP Configuration

Computers may be set up to receive network configuration dynamically. This allows a computer to request an address from a pool of addresses assigned by another device within the network. When the computer is finished with the address it is returned to the pool for assignment to another computer.

2.2.4 Computer Naming

Refer to
Figure
in online course

In addition to the IP address, some network operating systems make use of names. In this environment each individual system must have a unique name assigned to it.

A *computer name* provides a user friendly name, making it easier for users to connect to shared resources such as folders and printers on other computers.

The network administrator should determine a logical naming scheme that helps to identify a device's type and/or its location. For example, the name PRT-CL-Eng-01 could represent the first color laser printer in the Engineering Department.

These names are manually assigned to each device, although some tools do exist to help automate the naming process. A computer description can also be entered when assigning a name to provide additional information on the location or function of the device.

2.2.5 Network Name and Address Planning

Refer to
Figure
in online course

As a network grows in size and complexity, it becomes increasingly important that it is well planned, logically organized and well documented.

Many organizations develop conventions for naming and addressing of computers. These provide guidelines and rules that can be used by network support personnel when performing these tasks. Computer names must be unique and should have a consistent format that conveys meaningful information. This can help to determine device type, function, location and sequence number based on the device name. IP addresses must also be unique to each device.

The use of logical device naming and addressing conventions that are well documented can greatly simplify the task of training, network management and can help with *troubleshooting* when problems arise.

2.3   Maintaining the Operating System

2.3.1   Why and When to Apply Patches

Refer to
Figure
in online course

Once an operating system (OS) or application is installed, it is important to keep it up to date with the latest patches.

A patch is a piece of program code that can correct a problem or enhance the functionality of an application program or OS. They are usually provided by the manufacturer to repair a known vulnerability or reported problem.

Computers should be continually updated with the latest patches unless there is a good reason not to do so. Sometimes patches may negatively impact the operation of another system feature. The impact of the patch should be clearly understood before it is applied. This information can usually be found on the software manufacturer's web site.

2.3.2   Applying OS Patches

Refer to
Figure
in online course

Patches to operating systems can be installed in different ways, depending on the OS and the needs of the user. Options for downloading and installing updates include:

Automatic installation

The OS can be configured to connect to the manufacturer's web site, download and install minor updates without any user intervention. Updates can be scheduled to occur during times when the computer is on, but not in use.

Prompt for Permission

Some users wish to have control over which patches are applied. This is often the choice of users who understand what impact a patch may have on system performance. The system can be configured to notify the end-user when a patch is available. The user must then decide if the patch should be downloaded and installed.

Manual

Updates that require major pieces of code to be replaced on a system should be run manually. These major updates are often called service packs and are designed to correct problems with an application or OS, and sometimes to add functionality. These service packs usually require the end user to manually connect to a web site, download and install the update. They may also be installed from a CD that can be obtained from the manufacturer.

2.3.3   Applications Patches and Updates

Refer to
Figure
in online course

Refer to
Figure
in online course

Applications also require patches and updates. Patches are usually released by the manufacturer, to repair a detected vulnerability in the application that could lead to undesirable behavior.

Browsers and office software such as word processors, spreadsheet and database applications are common targets for network attacks. These applications require updates to correct the code that may allow the attack to succeed. The manufacturer may also develop updates that can improve product functionality, at no additional cost.

OS and applications patches are generally found through the manufacturer's website. The installation process may request permission to install the update and to verify that any supporting software is present. The installation process may also install any programs that are required to support the update. Web updates can be downloaded to the system from the Internet and installed automatically.

Refer to
Lab Activity
for this chapter

Lab Activity

Examine the current version of OS and installed application and determine whether additional patches or updates are available.

Summary

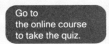

Quiz

Take the chapter quiz to check your knowledge.

Your Chapter Notes

CHAPTER 3

Connecting to the Network

Introduction

Refer to **Figure** in online course

3.1 Introduction to Networking

3.1.1 What is a Network?

Refer to **Figure** in online course

There are many types of networks that provide us with different kinds of services. In the course of a day, a person might make a phone call, watch a television show, listen to the radio, look up something on the Internet, or even play a video game with someone in another country. All of these activities depend on robust, reliable networks. Networks provide the ability to connect people and equipment no matter where they are in the world. People use networks without ever thinking about how they work or what it would be like if the networks did not exist.

This picture of the airport illustrates people using networks to share information, use resources and communicate with others. There are multiple types of networks shown in this scene. How many can you find?

Refer to **Figure** in online course

Communication technology in the 1990s, and before, required separate, dedicated networks for voice, video and computer data communications. Each of these networks required a different type of device in order to access the network. Telephones, televisions, and computers used specific technologies and different dedicated network structures, to communicate. But what if people want to access all of these network services at the same time, possibly using a single device?

New technologies create a new kind of network that delivers more than a single type of service. Unlike dedicated networks, these new converged networks are capable of delivering voice, video and data services over the same communication channel or network structure.

New products are coming to market that take advantage of the capabilities of converged information networks. People can now watch live video broadcasts on their computers, make a telephone call over the Internet, or search the Internet using a television. Converged networks make this possible.

In this course, the term network refers to these new multi-purpose, converged information networks.

3.1.2 Benefits of Networking

Refer to **Figure** in online course

Networks come in all sizes. They can range from simple networks consisting of two computers, to networks connecting millions of devices. Networks installed in small offices, or homes and home offices, are referred to as *SOHO* networks. SOHO networks enable sharing of resources, such as printers, documents, pictures and music between a few local computers.

In business, large networks can be used to advertise and sell products, order supplies, and communicate with customers. Communication over a network is usually more efficient and less expensive than traditional forms of communication, such as regular mail or long distance phone calls. Networks allow for rapid communication such as email and instant messaging, and provide consolidation, storage, and access to information on network servers.

Business and SOHO networks usually provide a shared connection to the Internet. The Internet is considered a "network of networks" because it is literally made up of thousands of networks that are connected to each other.

Here are other uses of a network and the Internet:

- Sharing music and video files
- Research and on-line learning
- Chatting with friends
- Planning vacations
- Purchasing gifts and supplies

Can you think of other ways people use networks and the Internet in their daily lives?

3.1.3 Basic Network Components

Refer to
Figure
in online course

There are many components that can be part of a network, for example personal computers, servers, networking devices, and cabling. These components can be grouped into four main categories:

- Hosts
- Shared peripherals
- Networking devices
- Networking media

The network components that people are most familiar with are hosts and shared peripherals. Hosts are devices that send and receive messages directly across the network.

Shared peripherals are not directly connected to the network, but instead are connected to hosts. The host is then responsible for sharing the peripheral across the network. Hosts have computer software configured to enable people on the network to use the attached peripheral devices.

The network devices, as well as networking media, are used to interconnect hosts.

Some devices can play more than one role, depending on how they are connected. For example, a printer directly connected to a host (local printer) is a peripheral. A printer directly connected to a network device and participates directly in network communications is a host.

Refer to
Interactive Graphic
in online course.

Activity

Identify the network components.

Scenario: Rakesh has decided to download some new songs on his MP3 player. He also wants to connect his game console to his network to play games with a friend in another city.

Drag the highlighted components to the appropriate categories.

3.1.4 Computer Roles in a Network

Refer to
Figure
in online course

All computers connected to a network that participate directly in network communication are classified as hosts. Hosts can send and receive messages on the network. In modern networks, computer hosts can act as a *client*, a server, or both. The software installed on the computer determines which role the computer plays.

Servers are hosts that have software installed that enable them to provide information, like email or web pages, to other hosts on the network. Each service requires separate server software. For example, a host requires web server software in order to provide web services to the network.

Clients are computer hosts that have software installed that enable them to request and display the information obtained from the server. An example of client software is a web browser, like Internet Explorer.

Refer to
Figure
in online course

A computer with server software can provide services simultaneously to one or many clients.

Additionally, a single computer can run multiple types of server software. In a home or small business, it may be necessary for one computer to act as a file server, a web server, and an email server.

A single computer can also run multiple types of client software. There must be client software for every service required. With multiple clients installed, a host can connect to multiple servers at the same time. For example, a user can check email and view a web page while instant messaging and listening to Internet radio.

Refer to
Interactive Graphic
in online course.

Activity

Match the client capabilities to the appropriate server(s).

Drag the client computer to the server(s) that have the appropriate server software to enable them to communicate.

3.1.5 Peer-to-Peer Networks

Refer to
Figure
in online course

Client and server software usually runs on separate computers, but it is also possible for one computer to carry out both roles at the same time. In small businesses and homes, many computers function as the servers and clients on the network. This type of network is called a peer-to-peer network.

The simplest peer-to-peer network consists of two directly connected computers using a wired or wireless connection.

Multiple PCs can also be connected to create a larger peer-to-peer network but this requires a *network device*, such as a *hub*, to interconnect the computers.

The main disadvantage of a peer-to-peer environment is that the performance of a host can be slowed down if it is acting as both a client and a server at the same time.

In larger businesses, due to the potential for high amounts of network traffic, it is often necessary to have dedicated servers to support the number of service requests.

Refer to
Interactive Graphic
in online course.

Activity

Identify if the computer is acting as a server, a client, or both for each scenario.

Click the appropriate role of client, server or both.

Refer to
Lab Activity
for this chapter

Lab Activity

Build a simple peer-to-peer network using two PCs and an Ethernet crossover cable.

3.1.6 Network Topologies

Refer to
Figure
in online course

In a simple network consisting of a few computers, it is easy to visualize how all of the various components connect. As networks grow, it is more difficult to keep track of the location of each component, and how each is connected to the network. Wired networks require lots of cabling and network devices to provide connectivity for all network hosts.

When networks are installed, a physical topology map is created to record where each host is located and how it is connected to the network. The physical topology map also shows where the wiring is installed and the locations of the networking devices that connect the hosts. Icons are used to represent the actual physical devices within the topology map. It is very important to maintain and update physical topology maps to aid future installation and troubleshooting efforts.

In addition to the physical topology map, it is sometimes necessary to also have a logical view of the network topology. A logical topology map groups hosts by how they use the network, no matter where they are physically located. Host names, addresses, group information and applications can be recorded on the logical topology map.

The graphics illustrate the difference between logical and physical topology maps.

3.2   Principles of Communication
3.2.1   Source, Channel, and Destination

Refer to
Figure
in online course

The primary purpose of any network is to provide a method to communicate information. From the very earliest primitive humans to the most advanced scientists of today, sharing information with others is crucial for human advancement.

All communication begins with a message, or information, that must be sent from one individual or device to another. The methods used to send, receive and interpret messages change over time as technology advances.

All communication methods have three elements in common. The first of these elements is the message source, or *sender*. Message sources are people, or electronic devices, that need to communicate a message to other individuals or devices. The second element of communication is the destination, or *receiver*, of the message. The destination receives the message and interprets it. A third element, called a channel, provides the pathway over which the message can travel from source to destination.

3.2.2   Rules of Communication

Refer to
Figure
in online course

In any conversation between two people, there are many rules, or protocols, that the two must follow in order for the message to be successfully delivered and understood. Among the protocols for successful human communication are:

- Identification of sender and receiver
- Agreed-upon medium or channel (face-to-face, telephone, letter, photograph)

- Appropriate communication mode (spoken, written, illustrated, interactive or one-way)

- Common language

- Grammar and sentence structure

- Speed and timing of delivery

Imagine what would happen if no protocols or rules existed to govern how people communicate with each other. Would you be able to understand them? Are you able to read the paragraph that does not follow commonly accepted protocols?

Refer to **Figure** in online course

Protocols are specific to the characteristics of the source, channel and destination of the message. The rules used to communicate over one medium, like a telephone call, are not necessarily the same as communication using another medium, such as a letter.

Protocols define the details of how the message is transmitted, and delivered. This includes issues of:

- Message format

- Message size

- Timing

- Encapsulation

- Encoding

- Standard message pattern

Many of the concepts and rules that make human communication reliable and understandable also apply to computer communication.

3.2.3 Message Encoding

Refer to **Figure** in online course

One of the first steps to sending a message is encoding it. Written words, pictures, and spoken languages each use a unique set of codes, sounds, gestures, and/or symbols to represent the thoughts being shared. Encoding is the process of converting thoughts into the language, symbols, or sounds, for transmission. Decoding reverses this process in order to interpret the thought.

Imagine a person watching a sunset and then calling someone else to talk about how beautiful the sunset looks. To communicate the message, the sender must first convert, or encode, their thoughts and perceptions about the sunset into words. The words are spoken into the telephone using the sounds and inflections of spoken language that convey the message. On the other end of the telephone line, the person listening to the description, receives and decodes the sounds in order to visualize the image of the sunset described by the sender.

Encoding also occurs in computer communication. Encoding between hosts must be in an appropriate form for the medium. Messages sent across the network are first converted into bits by the sending host. Each bit is encoded into a pattern of sounds, light waves, or electrical impulses depending on the network media over which the bits are transmitted. The *destination host* receives and decodes the signals in order to interpret the message.

3.2.4 Message Formatting

Refer to **Figure** in online course

When a message is sent from source to destination, it must use a specific format or structure. Message formats depend on the type of message and the channel that is used to deliver the message.

Letter writing is one of the most common forms of written human communication. For centuries, the agreed format for personal letters has not changed. In many cultures, a personal letter contains the following elements:

- An identifier of the recipient

- A salutation or greeting

- The message content

- A closing phrase

- An identifier of the sender

In addition to having the correct format, most personal letters must also be enclosed, or encapsulated, in an envelope for delivery. The envelope has the address of the sender and receiver on it, each located at the proper place on the envelope. If the destination address and formatting are not correct, the letter is not delivered.

The process of placing one message format (the letter) inside another message format (the envelope) is called encapsulation. De-encapsulation occurs when the process is reversed by the recipient and the letter is removed from the envelope.

Refer to
Figure
in online course

A letter writer uses an accepted format to ensure that the letter is delivered and understood by the recipient. In the same way, a message that is sent over a computer network follows specific format rules for it to be delivered and processed. Just as a letter is encapsulated in an envelope for delivery, so computer messages are encapsulated. Each computer message is encapsulated in a specific format, called a *frame*, before it is sent over the network. A frame acts like an envelope; it provides the address of the intended destination and the address of the source host.

The format and contents of a frame are determined by the type of message being sent and the channel over which it is communicated. Messages that are not correctly formatted are not successfully delivered to or processed by the destination host.

Refer to
Interactive Graphic
in online course.

Activity

Place the components of a voice message into the proper location within a frame.

Voice Message: Christopher calls his friend Tasha and leaves her a voice message about their homework assignment. The telephone number for Tasha is 999-555-1000 and for Christopher, 999-555-2000.

The voice message is "Hello Tasha, this is Christopher. Can you tell me what today's math assignment is? Thanks, bye."

Drag the voice message components to the proper location within the frame.

3.2.5 Message Size

Refer to
Figure
in online course

Imagine what it would be like to read this course if it all appeared as one long sentence; it would not be easy to read and comprehend. When people communicate with each other, the messages that they send are usually broken into smaller parts or sentences. These sentences are limited in size to what the receiving person can process at one time. An individual conversation may be made up of many smaller sentences to ensure that each part of the message is received and understood.

Likewise, when a long message is sent from one host to another over a network, it is necessary to break the message into smaller pieces. The rules that govern the size of the pieces, or frames, communicated across the network are very strict. They can also be different, depending on the channel used. Frames that are too long or too short are not delivered.

The size restrictions of frames require the source host to break a long message into individual pieces that meet both the minimum and maximum size requirements. Each piece is encapsulated in a separate frame with the address information, and is sent over the network. At the receiving host, the messages are de-encapsulated and put back together to be processed and interpreted.

3.2.6 Message Timing

Refer to **Figure** in online course

One factor that affects how well a message is received and understood is timing. People use timing to determine when to speak, how fast or slow to talk, and how long to wait for a response. These are the rules of engagement.

Access Method

Access Method determines when someone is able to send a message. These timing rules are based on the environment. For example, you may be able to speak whenever you have something to say. In this environment, a person must wait until no one else is talking before speaking. If two people talk at the same time, a *collision* of information occurs and it is necessary for the two to back off and start again. These rules ensure communication is successful. Likewise, it is necessary for computers to define an *access method*. Hosts on a network need an access method to know when to begin sending messages and how to respond when errors occur.

Flow Control

Timing also effects how much information can be sent and the speed that it can be delivered. If one person speaks too quickly, it is difficult for the other person to hear and understand the message. The receiving person must ask the sender to slow down. In network communication, a sending host can transmit messages at a faster rate than the destination host can receive and process. Source and destination hosts use flow control to negotiate correct timing for successful communication.

Response Timeout

If a person asks a question and does not hear a response within an acceptable amount of time, the person assumes that no answer is coming and reacts accordingly. The person may repeat the question, or may go on with the conversation. Hosts on the network also have rules that specify how long to wait for responses and what action to take if a response timeout occurs.

3.2.7 Message Patterns

Refer to **Figure** in online course

Sometimes, a person wants to communicate information to a single individual. At other times, the person may need to send information to a group of people at the same time, or even to all people in the same area. A conversation between two people is an example of a one-to-one pattern of communication. When a group of recipients need to receive the same message simultaneously, a one-to-many or one-to-all message pattern is necessary.

There are also times when the sender of a message needs to be sure that the message is delivered successfully to the destination. In these cases, it is necessary for the recipient to return an acknowledgement to the sender. If no acknowledgement is required, the message pattern is referred to as unacknowledged.

Hosts on a network use similar message patterns to communicate.

A one-to-one message pattern is referred to as a *unicast*, meaning that there is only a single destination for the message.

When a host needs to send messages using a one-to-many pattern, it is referred to as a *multicast*. Multicasting is the delivery of the same message to a group of host destinations simultaneously.

If all hosts on the network need to receive the message at the same time, a *broadcast* is used. Broadcasting represents a one-to-all message pattern. Additionally, hosts have requirements for acknowledged versus unacknowledged messages.

3.2.8 Protocol Use in Communication

Refer to
Figure
in online course

All communication, both human and computer, is governed by pre-established rules, or protocols. These protocols are determined by the characteristics of the source, channel and destination. Based on the source, channel and destination, the protocols define the details for the issues of message format, message size, timing, encapsulation, encoding and standard message pattern.

Refer to
Interactive Graphic
in online course.

Activity

Determine if the communication problem described deals with encoding, message format, timing, unit size, or message pattern.

Drag the communication characteristic producing the problem to the appropriate scenario.

3.3 Communicating on a Local Wired Network

3.3.1 Importance of Protocols

Refer to
Figure
in online course

Computers, just like humans, use rules, or protocols, in order to communicate.

Protocols are especially important on a local network. In a wired environment, a local network is defined as an area where all hosts must "speak the same language" or in computer terms "share a common protocol".

If everyone in the same room spoke a different language they would not be able to communicate. Likewise, if devices in a local network did not use the same protocols they would not be able to communicate.

The most common set of protocols used on local wired networks is Ethernet.

The Ethernet protocol defines many aspects of communication over the local network, including: message format, message size, timing, encoding, and message patterns.

3.3.2 Standardization of Protocols

Refer to
Figure
in online course

In the early days of networking, each vendor used their own, proprietary methods of interconnecting network devices and networking protocols. Equipment from one vendor could not communicate with equipment from another.

As networks became more widespread, standards were developed that defined rules by which network equipment from different vendors operated. Standards are beneficial to networking in many ways:

■ Facilitate design

- Simplify product development

- Promote competition

- Provide consistent interconnections

- Facilitate training

- Provide more vendor choices for customers

There is no official local networking standard protocol, but over time, one technology, Ethernet, has become more common than the others. It has become a *de facto standard*.

Refer to **Figure** in online course

The Institute of Electrical and Electronic Engineers, or *IEEE* (pronounced eye-triple-e), maintains the networking standards, including Ethernet and wireless standards. IEEE committees are responsible for approving and maintaining the standards for connections, media requirements and communications protocols. Each technology standard is assigned a number that refers to the committee that is responsible for approving and maintaining the standard. The committee responsible for the Ethernet standards is 802.3.

Since the creation of Ethernet in 1973, standards have evolved for specifying faster and more flexible versions of the technology. This ability for Ethernet to improve over time is one of the main reasons that it has become so popular. Each version of Ethernet has an associated standard. For example, 802.3 100BASE-T represents the 100 Megabit Ethernet using twisted pair cable standards. The standard notation translates as:

- 100 is the speed in Mbps

- BASE stands for *baseband* transmission

- T stands for the type of cable, in this case, twisted pair.

Early versions of Ethernet were relatively slow at 10 Mbps. The latest versions of Ethernet operate at 10 Gigabits per second and faster. Imagine how much faster these new versions are than the original Ethernet networks.

3.3.3 Physical Addressing

Refer to **Figure** in online course

All communication requires a way to identify the source and destination. The source and destination in human communication are represented by names.

When a name is called, the person with that name listens to the message and responds. Other people in the room may hear the message, but they ignore it because it is not addressed to them.

On Ethernet networks, a similar method exists for identifying source and destination hosts. Each host connected to an Ethernet network is assigned a physical address which serves to identify the host on the network.

Every Ethernet network interface has a physical address assigned to it when it is manufactured. This address is known as the Media Access Control (MAC) Address. The *MAC address* identifies each source and destination host on the network.

Ethernet networks are cable based, meaning that a copper or fiber optic cable connects hosts and networking devices. This is the channel used for communications between the hosts.

When a host on an Ethernet network communicates, it sends frames containing its own MAC address as the source and the MAC address of the intended recipient. Any hosts that receive the frame will *decode* the frame and read the destination MAC address. If the destination MAC address matches the address configured on the NIC, it will process the message and store it for the host application to use. If the destination MAC address does not match the host MAC address, the NIC will ignore the message.

Refer to
Lab Activity
for this chapter

Lab Activity

Use the *ipconfig* /all command to display the MAC address of your computer.

3.3.4 Ethernet Communication

Refer to
Figure
in online course

The Ethernet protocol standards define many aspects of network communication including frame format, frame size, timing and encoding.

When messages are sent between hosts on an Ethernet network, the hosts format the messages into the frame layout that is specified by the standards. Frames are also referred to as Protocol Data Units (PDUs).

The format for Ethernet frames specifies the location of the destination and source MAC addresses, and additional information including:

- Preamble for sequencing and timing
- Start of frame delimiter
- Length and type of frame
- Frame check sequence to detect transmission errors

The size of Ethernet frames is limited to a maximum of 1518 bytes and a minimum size of 64 bytes from the Destination MAC Address field through the Frame Check Sequence. Frames that do not match these limits are not processed by the receiving hosts. In addition to the frame formats, sizes and timing, Ethernet standards define how the bits making up the frames are encoded onto the channel. Bits are transmitted as either electrical impulses over copper cable or as light impulses over fiber optic cable.

Refer to
Interactive Graphic
in online course.

Activity

Build a standard IEEE 802.3 Ethernet frame based on the source and the destination device.

Drag the components to their proper location within the Ethernet frame based on the source and destination devices.

3.3.5 Hierarchical Design of Ethernet Networks

Refer to
Figure
in online course

Imagine how difficult communication would be if the only way to send a message to someone was to use the person's name. If there were no street addresses, cities, towns, or country boundaries, delivering a message to a specific person across the world would be nearly impossible.

On an Ethernet network, the host MAC address is similar to a person's name. A MAC address indicates the individual identity of a specific host, but it does not indicate where on the network the host is located. If all hosts on the Internet (over 400 million of them) were each identified by only their unique MAC address, imagine how difficult it would be to locate a single one.

Additionally, Ethernet technology generates a large amount of broadcast traffic in order for hosts to communicate. Broadcasts are sent to all hosts within a single network. Broadcasts consume bandwidth and slow network performance. What would happen if the millions of hosts attached to the Internet were all in one Ethernet network and were using broadcasts?

For these two reasons, large Ethernet networks consisting of many hosts are not efficient. It is better to divide larger networks into smaller, more manageable pieces. One way to divide larger networks is to use a hierarchical design model.

Refer to
Figure
in online course

In networking, hierarchical design is used to group devices into multiple networks that are organized in a layered approach. It consists of smaller, more manageable groups that allow local traffic to remain local. Only traffic that is destined for other networks is moved to a higher layer.

A hierarchical, layered design provides increased efficiency, optimization of function, and increased speed. It allows the network to scale as required because additional local networks can be added without impacting the performance of the existing ones.

The hierarchical design has three basic layers:

- *Access Layer -* to provide connections to hosts in a local Ethernet network.
- *Distribution Layer -* to interconnect the smaller local networks.
- *Core Layer -* a high-speed connection between distribution layer devices.

With this new hierarchical design, there is a need for a logical addressing scheme that can identify the location of a host. This is the Internet Protocol (IP) addressing scheme.

3.3.6 Logical Addressing

Refer to
Figure
in online course

A person's name usually does not change. A person's address on the other hand, relates to where they live and can change. On a host, the MAC address does not change; it is physically assigned to the host NIC and is known as the physical address. The physical address remains the same regardless of where the host is placed on the network.

The IP address is similar to the address of a person. It is known as a *logical address* because it is assigned logically based on where the host is located. The IP address, or *network address*, is assigned to each host by a network administrator based on the local network.

IP addresses contain two parts. One part identifies the local network. The network portion of the IP address will be the same for all hosts connected to the same local network. The second part of the IP address identifies the individual host. Within the same local network, the host portion of the IP address is unique to each host.

Both the physical MAC and logical IP addresses are required for a computer to communicate on a hierarchical network, just like both the name and address of a person are required to send a letter.

Refer to
Lab Activity
for this chapter

Lab Activity

Use the `ipconfig /all` command to display the IP address of your computer.

3.3.7 Access and Distribution Layers and Devices

Refer to
Figure
in online course

IP traffic is managed based on the characteristics and devices associated with each of the three layers: Access, Distribution and Core. The IP address is used to determine if traffic should remain local or be moved up through the layers of the hierarchical network.

Access Layer

The Access Layer provides a connection point for end user devices to the network and allows multiple hosts to connect to other hosts through a network device, usually a hub or switch. Typically, all devices within a single Access Layer will have the same network portion of the IP address.

If a message is destined for a local host, based on the network portion of the IP address, the message remains local. If it is destined for a different network, it is passed up to the Distribution Layer. Hubs and switches provide the connection to the Distribution Layer devices, usually a router.

Distribution Layer

The Distribution Layer provides a connection point for separate networks and controls the flow of information between the networks. It typically contains more powerful switches than the Access Layer as well as routers for *routing* between networks. Distribution Layer devices control the type and amount of traffic that flows from the Access Layer to the Core Layer.

Core Layer

The Core Layer is a high-speed backbone layer with redundant (backup) connections. It is responsible for transporting large amounts of data between multiple end networks. Core Layer devices typically include very powerful, high-speed switches and routers. The main goal of the Core Layer is to transport data quickly.

Hubs, switches, and routers are discussed in more detail in the next two sections.

Activity

> Refer to
> **Interactive Graphic**
> in online course.

Determine which addresses, network components and layers are necessary to accomplish each task.

For each scenario, click the box next to each component required to complete the task.

3.4 Building the Access Layer of an Ethernet Network

3.4.1 Access Layer

> Refer to
> **Figure**
> in online course

The Access Layer is the most basic level of the network. It is the part of the network in which people gain access to other hosts and to shared files and printers. The Access Layer is composed of host devices, as well as the first line of networking devices to which they are attached.

Networking devices enable us to connect many hosts with each other and also provide those hosts access to services offered over the network. Unlike the simple network consisting of two hosts connected by a single cable, in the Access Layer, each host is connected to a networking device. This type of connectivity is shown in the graphic.

Within an Ethernet network, each host is able to connect directly to an Access Layer networking device using a point-to-point cable. These cables are manufactured to meet specific Ethernet standards. Each cable is plugged into a host NIC and then into a port on the networking device. There are several types of networking devices that can be used to connect hosts at the Access Layer, including Ethernet hubs and switches.

3.4.2 Function of Hubs

> Refer to
> **Figure**
> in online course

A hub is one type of networking device that is installed at the Access Layer of an Ethernet network. Hubs contain multiple ports that are used to connect hosts to the network. Hubs are simple devices that do not have the necessary electronics to decode the messages sent between hosts on the network. Hubs cannot determine which host should get any particular message. A hub simply accepts electronic signals from one port and regenerates (or repeats) the same message out all of the other ports.

Remember that the NIC on a host accepts messages only addressed to the correct MAC address. Hosts ignore messages that are not addressed to them. Only the host specified in the destination address of the message processes the message and responds to the sender.

All of the ports on the Ethernet hub connect to the same channel to send and receive messages. Because all hosts must share the bandwidth available on that channel, a hub is referred to as a shared-bandwidth device.

Refer to
Figure
in online course

Only one message can be sent through an Ethernet hub at a time. It is possible for two or more hosts connected to a hub to attempt to send a message at the same time. If this happens, the electronic signals that make up the messages collide with each other at the hub.

A collision causes the messages to become garbled and unreadable by the hosts. A hub does not decode the messages; therefore it does not detect that the message is garbled and repeats it out all the ports. The area of the network where a host can receive a garbled message resulting from a collision is known as a *collision domain*.

Inside a collision domain, when a host receives a garbled message, it detects that a collision has occurred. Each sending host waits a short amount of time and then attempts to send, or retransmit, the message again. As the number of hosts connected to the hub increases, so does the chance of collisions. More collisions cause more retransmissions. Excessive retransmissions can clog up the network and slow down network traffic. For this reason, it is necessary to limit the size of a collision domain.

Refer to
Interactive Graphic
in online course.

Activity

Answer a series of questions based on your observation of traffic through a hub network.

3.4.3 Function of Switches

Refer to
Figure
in online course

An Ethernet switch is a device that is used at the Access Layer. Like a hub, a switch connects multiple hosts to the network. Unlike a hub, a switch can forward a message to a specific host. When a host sends a message to another host on the switch, the switch accepts and decodes the frames to read the physical (MAC) address portion of the message.

A table on the switch, called a MAC address table, contains a list of all of the active ports and the host MAC addresses that are attached to them. When a message is sent between hosts, the switch checks to see if the destination MAC address is in the table. If it is, the switch builds a temporary connection, called a circuit, between the source and destination ports. This new circuit provides a dedicated channel over which the two hosts can communicate. Other hosts attached to the switch do not share bandwidth on this channel and do not receive messages that are not addressed to them. A new circuit is built for every new conversation between hosts. These separate circuits allow many conversations to take place at the same time, without collisions occurring.

Refer to
Figure
in online course

What happens when the switch receives a frame addressed to a new host that is not yet in the MAC address table? If the destination MAC address is not in the table, the switch does not have the necessary information to create an individual circuit. When the switch cannot determine where the destination host is located, it uses a process called flooding to forward the message out to all attached hosts. Each host compares the destination MAC address in the message to its own MAC address, but only the host with the correct destination address processes the message and responds to the sender.

How does the MAC address of a new host get into the MAC address table? A switch builds the MAC address table by examining the source MAC address of each frame that is sent between hosts. When a new host sends a message or responds to a flooded message, the switch immediately learns its MAC address and the port to which it is connected. The table is dynamically updated each time a new source MAC address is read by the switch. In this way, a switch quickly learns the MAC addresses of all attached hosts.

Refer to
Figure
in online course

Sometimes, it is necessary to connect another networking device, like a hub, to a switch port. This is done to increase the number of hosts that can be connected to the network. When a hub is connected to a switch port, the switch associates the MAC addresses of all hosts connected to that hub with the single port on the switch. Occasionally, one host on the attached hub sends a message to another host attached to the same hub. In this case, the switch receives the frame and checks the table to see where the destination host is located. If both the source and destination hosts are located on the same port, the switch discards the message.

When a hub is connected to a switch port, collisions can occur on the hub. The hub forwards to all ports the damaged messages resulting from a collision. The switch receives the garbled message, but, unlike a hub, a switch does not forward the damaged messages caused by collisions. As a result, every switch port creates a separate collision domain. This is a good thing. The fewer hosts contained in a collision domain, the less likely it is that a collision will occur.

Refer to
Interactive Graphic
in online course.

Activity

Answer a series of questions based on your observation of traffic through a combination switch and hub network.

3.4.4 Broadcast Messaging

Refer to
Figure
in online course

When hosts are connected using either a hub or a switch, a single local network is created. Within the local network it is often necessary for one host to be able to send messages to all the other hosts at the same time. This can be done using a message known as a broadcast. Broadcasts are useful when a host needs to find information without knowing exactly what other host can supply it or when a host wants to provide information to all other hosts in the same network in a timely manner.

A message can only contain one destination MAC address. So, how is it possible for a host to contact every other host on the local network without sending out a separate message to each individual MAC?

To solve this problem, broadcast messages are sent to a unique MAC address that is recognized by all hosts. The *broadcast MAC address* is actually a 48-bit address made up of all ones. Because of their length, MAC addresses are usually represented in *hexadecimal* notation. The broadcast MAC address in hexadecimal notation is FFFF.FFFF.FFFF. Each F in the hexadecimal notation represents four ones in the binary address.

Refer to
Figure
in online course

When a host receives a message addressed to the broadcast address, it accepts and processes the message as though the message was addressed directly to it. When a host sends a broadcast message, hubs and switches forward the message to every connected host within the same local network. For this reason, a local network is also referred to as a *broadcast domain*.

If too many hosts are connected to the same broadcast domain, broadcast traffic can become excessive. The number of hosts and the amount of network traffic that can be supported on the local network is limited by the capabilities of the hubs and switches used to connect them. As the network grows and more hosts are added, network traffic, including broadcast traffic, increases. It is often necessary to divide one local network, or broadcast domain, into multiple networks to improve performance.

3.4.5 Switch Behavior

Refer to
Interactive Graphic
in online course.

Activity

In this activity, determine how the switch forwards a frame based on the Source MAC and Destination MAC addresses and information in the switch *MAC table*.

3.4.6 MAC and IP

Refer to
Figure
in online course

On a local Ethernet network, a NIC only accepts a frame if the destination address is either the broadcast MAC address, or else corresponds to the MAC address of the NIC.

Most network applications, however, rely on the logical destination IP address to identify the location of the servers and clients.

What if a sending host only has the logical IP address of the destination host? How does the sending host determine what destination MAC address to place within the frame?

The sending host can use an IP protocol called address resolution protocol (ARP) to discover the MAC address of any host on the same local network.

3.4.7 Address Resolution Protocol (ARP)

Refer to
Figure
in online course

ARP uses a three step process to discover and store the MAC address of a host on the local network when only the IP address of the host is known.

> **Step 1.**   The sending host creates and sends a frame addressed to a broadcast MAC address. Contained in the frame is a message with the IP address of the intended destination host.
>
> **Step 2.**   Each host on the network receives the broadcast frame and compares the IP address inside the message with its configured IP address. The host with the matching IP address sends its MAC address back to the original sending host.
>
> **Step 3.**   The sending host receives the message and stores the MAC address and IP address information in a table called an ARP table.

Once the sending host has the MAC address of the destination host in its ARP table, it can send frames directly to the destination without doing an ARP request.

3.5 Building the Distribution Layer of Network

3.5.1 Distribution Layer

Refer to
Figure
in online course

As networks grow, it is often necessary to divide one local network into multiple Access Layer networks. There are many ways to divide networks based on different criteria, including:

- Physical location
- Logical function
- Security requirements
- Application requirements

The Distribution Layer connects these independent local networks and controls the traffic flowing between them. It is responsible for ensuring that traffic between hosts on the local network stays local. Only traffic that is destined for other networks is passed on. The Distribution Layer can also filter incoming and outgoing traffic for security and traffic management.

Networking devices that make up the Distribution Layer are designed to interconnect networks, not individual hosts. Individual hosts are connected to the network via Access Layer devices, such as hubs and switches. The Access Layer devices are connected to each other via the Distribution Layer device, such as routers.

3.5.2 Function of Routers

Refer to
Figure
in online course

A router is a networking device that connects a local network to other local networks. At the Distribution Layer of the network, routers direct traffic and perform other functions critical to efficient network operation. Routers, like switches, are able to decode and read the messages that are sent to them. Unlike switches, which only decode (unencapsulate) the frame containing the MAC address information, routers decode the *packet* that is encapsulated within the frame.

The packet format contains the IP addresses of the destination and source hosts, as well as the message data being sent between them. The router reads the network portion of the destination IP address and uses it to find which one of the attached networks is the best way to forward the message to the destination.

Anytime the network portion of the IP addresses of the source and destination hosts do not match, a router must be used to forward the message. If a host located on network 1.1.1.0 needs to send a message to a host on network 5.5.5.0, the host will forward the message to the router. The router receives the message and unencapsulates it to read the destination IP address. It then determines where to forward the message. It re-encapsulates the packet back into a frame, and forwards the frame on to its destination.

Refer to
Lab Activity
for this chapter

Lab Activity

Refer to
Figure
in online course

Assign different IP addresses on a peer-to-peer network, and view the effects on network communication.

How does the router determine what path to send the message to get to the destination network?

Each port, or interface, on a router connects to a different local network. Every router contains a table of all locally-connected networks and the interfaces that connect to them. These routing tables can also contain information about the routes, or paths, that the router uses to reach other remote networks that are not locally attached.

When a router receives a frame, it decodes the frame to get to the packet containing the destination IP address. It matches the address of the destination to all of the networks that are contained in the routing table. If the destination network address is in the table, the router encapsulates the packet in a new frame in order to send it out. It forwards the new frame out of the interface associated with the path, to the destination network. The process of forwarding the packets toward their destination network is called routing.

Router interfaces do not forward messages that are addressed to the local network broadcast IP address. As a result, local network broadcasts are not sent across routers to other local networks.

3.5.3 Default Gateway

Refer to
Figure
in online course

The method that a host uses to send messages to a destination on a remote network differs from the way a host sends messages on the same local network. When a host needs to send a message to another host located on the same network, it will forward the message directly. A host will use ARP to discover the MAC address of the destination host. It includes the destination IP address within the packet and encapsulates the packet into a frame containing the MAC address of the destination and forwards it out.

On the other hand, when a host needs to send a message to a remote network, it must use the router. The host includes the IP address of the destination host within the packet just like before. However, when it encapsulates the packet into a frame, it uses the MAC address of the router as the destination for the frame. In this way, the router will receive and accept the frame based on the MAC address.

How does the source host determine the MAC address of the router? A host is given the IP address of the router through the *default gateway* address configured in its TCP/IP settings. The default gateway address is the address of the router interface connected to the same local network as the source host. All hosts on the local network use the default gateway address to send messages to the router. Once the host knows the default gateway IP address, it can use ARP to determine the MAC address. The MAC address of the router is then placed in the frame, destined for another network.

It is important that the correct default gateway be configured on each host on the local network. If no default gateway is configured in the host TCP/IP settings, or if the wrong default gateway is specified, messages addressed to hosts on remote networks cannot be delivered.

Refer to **Interactive Graphic** in online course.

Activity

There are three local networks connected by a router. Use the TPC/IP configuration screen to enter the proper default gateway address for each PC.

Click each PC to enter the default gateway.

3.5.4 Tables Maintained by Routers

Refer to **Figure** in online course

Routers move information between local and remote networks. To do this, routers must use both ARP and routing tables to store information. Routing tables are not concerned with the addresses of individual hosts. Routing tables contain the addresses of networks and the best path to reach those networks. Entries can be made to the routing table in two ways: dynamically updated by information received from other routers in the network, or manually entered by a network administrator. Routers use the routing tables to determine which interface to use to forward a message to its intended destination.

If the router cannot determine where to forward a message, it will drop it. Network administrators configure a routing table with a default route to keep a packet from being dropped because the path to the destination network is not in the routing table. A default route is the interface through which the router forwards a packet containing an unknown destination IP network address. This default route usually connects to another router that can forward the packet towards its final destination network.

Refer to **Figure** in online course

A router forwards a frame to one of two places: a directly connected network containing the actual destination host, or to another router on the path to reach the destination host. When a router encapsulates the frame to forward it out of an Ethernet interface, it must include a destination MAC address.

This is the MAC address of the actual destination host, if the destination host is part of a network locally connected to the router. If the router must forward the packet to another router, it will use the MAC address of the connected router. Routers obtain these MAC addresses from ARP tables.

Each router interface is part of the local network to which it is attached and maintains its own ARP table for that network. The ARP tables contain the MAC addresses and IP addresses of all of the individual hosts on that network.

Refer to **Interactive Graphic** in online course.

Activity

Determine how the router forwards a packet based on the source and destination address and information in the route table.

Answer the questions based on the information in the graphic.

3.5.5 Local Area Network (LAN)

Refer to **Figure** in online course

The term Local Area Network (LAN) refers to a local network, or a group of interconnected local networks that are under the same administrative control. In the early days of networking, LANs were defined as small networks that existed in a single physical location. While LANs can be a single local network installed in a home or small office, the definition of LAN has evolved to include interconnected local networks consisting of many hundreds of hosts, installed in multiple buildings and locations.

The important thing to remember is that all of the local networks within a LAN are under one administrative control. Other common characteristics of LANs are that they typically use Ethernet or wireless protocols, and they support high data rates.

The term Intranet is often used to refer to a private LAN that belongs to an organization, and is designed to be accessible only by the organization's members, employees, or others with authorization.

Refer to Interactive Graphic in online course.

Activity

Identify the number of local networks within the LAN.

Count the local networks and enter the number in the space provided.

3.5.6 Adding Hosts to Local and Remote Networks

Refer to Figure in online course

Within a LAN, it is possible to place all hosts on a single local network or divide them up between multiple networks connected by a Distribution Layer. The answer depends on desired results. Placing all hosts on a single local network allows them to be seen by all other hosts. This is because there is one broadcast domain and hosts use ARP to find each other.

In a simple network design it may be beneficial to keep all hosts within a single local network. However, as networks grow in size, increased traffic will decrease network performance and speed. In this case, it may be beneficial to move some hosts onto a remote network.

Placing additional hosts on a remote network will decrease the impact of traffic demands. However, hosts on one network will not be able to communicate with hosts on the other without the use of routing. Routers increase the complexity of the network configuration and can introduce latency, or time delay, on packets sent from one local network to the other.

3.5.7 Learn to Use Packet Tracer

Refer to Figure in online course

Packet Tracer is a graphical learning and simulation tool Cisco developed to help model and understand how networks function. It enables you to build network topologies and test them by sending packets between devices and observing the interactions of protocols in use.

Click Play to view a tutorial.

Refer to Packet Tracer Activity for this chapter

Packet Tracer Activity

Become familiar with the user interface of Packet Tracer. Model a simple network and observe network behavior. Create an Ethernet network using two hosts and a hub and observe ARP, broadcast and *ping* (ICMP) traffic.

3.6 Plan and Connect a Local Network

3.6.1 Plan and Document an Ethernet Network

Refer to Figure in online course

Most local networks are based on Ethernet technology. This technology is both fast and efficient when used in a properly designed and constructed network. The key to installing a good network is planning before the network is actually built.

A network plan starts with the gathering of information about how the network will be used. This information includes:

- The number and type of hosts to be connected to network

- The applications to be used

- Sharing and Internet connectivity requirements

- Security and privacy considerations

- Reliability and uptime expectations

- Connectivity requirements including, wired and wireless

Refer to **Figure** in online course

There are many considerations that must be taken into account when planning for a network installation. The logical and physical topology maps of the network need to be designed and documented before the networking equipment is purchased and the hosts are connected. Some things to consider include:

Physical environment where the network will be installed:

- Temperature control: all devices have specific ranges of temperature and humidity requirements for proper operation

- Availability and placement of power outlets

Physical configuration of the network:

- Physical location of devices such as routers, switches, and hosts

- How all devices are interconnected

- Location and length of all cable runs

- Hardware configuration of end devices such as hosts and servers

Logical configuration of the network:

- Location and size of broadcast and collision domains

- IP addressing scheme

- Naming scheme

- Sharing configuration

- Permissions

3.6.2 Prototypes

Refer to **Figure** in online course

Once the network requirements are documented, and the physical and logical topology maps created, the next step in the implementation process is to test the network design. One of the ways to test a network design is to create a working model, or prototype, of the network.

Prototyping is essential as networks grow in size and complexity. A prototype allows a network administrator to test whether or not the planned network will operate as expected, before money is spent on equipment and installation. Documentation should be maintained on all aspects of the *prototyping* process.

Various tools and techniques are available for network prototyping; this includes real equipment set up in a lab environment, modeling and simulation tools. Packet Tracer is one example of a simulation and modeling tool that can be used for prototyping.

Refer to
Figure
in online course

Refer to **Packet
Tracer Activity**
for this chapter

Refer to
Figure
in online course

Packet Tracer Activity

Prototype a simple network consisting of two hosts and a switch.

3.6.3 Multi-function Device

Most home and small business networks do not require high-volume devices used in large business environments; smaller scale devices may well be suitable. However, the same functionality of routing and switching is required. This need has led to the development of products that have the functionality of multiple network devices, such as a router with switching functionality and a wireless *access point*. For the purpose of this course, multi-function devices will be referred to as integrated routers. Integrated routers can range from small devices designed for home office and small business applications to more powerful devices that can support enterprise branch offices.

An integrated router is like having several different devices connected together. For example, the connection between the switch and the router still occurs, but it occurs internally. When a broadcast is received on a switch port, the integrated router forwards the broadcast to all ports including the internal router connection. The router portion of the integrated router stops the broadcasts from going any further.

There are low-cost multi-function devices available for home and small business networks that offer integrated routing, switching, wireless and security capabilities. An example of this type of integrated router is a Linksys wireless router. They are simple in design and do not typically have separate components. In the event of a failure, it is not possible to replace any single failed component. As such, they create a single point of failure, and are not optimized for any one function.

Another example of an integrated router is the Cisco integrated services router or ISR. The Cisco ISR product family offers a wide range of products, including those designed for small office and home office environments as well as those designed for larger networks. Many of the ISRs offer modularity and have separate components for each function, such as a switch component and a router component. This enables individual components to be added, replaced and upgraded as necessary.

3.6.4 Connecting the Linksys Router

Refer to
Figure
in online course

Front View:

The Linksys is a simplified, low-cost device that carries out the functionality of multiple network devices (switch, router, wireless access point).

Light emitting diodes (LEDs) indicate the connection status of each port.

Click the LEDs for a description.

Refer to
Figure
in online course

All devices connected to the switch ports should be in the same broadcast domain. This means that all devices must have an IP address from the same network. Any device that has a different network portion within the IP address will not be able to communicate.

Additionally, Microsoft Windows makes use of computer names to identify other devices on the network. It is important to use these names as well as all IP address information in the planning and documentation to assist in future troubleshooting.

To display the current IP configuration in Microsoft Windows, use the command `ipconfig`. More detailed information, including host name, is available with the `ipconfig /all`. Document all information from the connection and configuration process.

Once hosts are communicating across the network, it is important to document network performance. This is known as determining the *baseline* for the network, and is used as an indication of normal operations. When comparing future network performance with the baseline, it can indicate if possible issues exist.

Refer to
Lab Activity
for this chapter

Lab Activity

Build and document a simple pre-planned network using a networking device and two hosts and verify IP configuration.

3.6.5 Sharing Resources

Refer to
Figure
in online course

One of the most common purposes of networking is to share resources such as files and printers. Windows XP enables remote users to access a local machine and its resources through Sharing. It is important to consider security issues, and to assign specific permissions to shared resources.

By default, Windows XP uses a process known as Simple File Sharing. With Simple File Sharing, specific users and groups cannot be prevented from accessing shared files.

Simple File Sharing can be disabled so that more specific security access levels can be assigned. When this is done, the following permissions are available to assign to resources:

- Full Control
- Modify
- Read & Execute
- List Folder Contents
- Read
- Write

Refer to
Figure
in online course

When a user accesses a file on a remote device, Windows Explorer allows the user to map a drive to a remote folder or resource. This maps a specific drive letter, for example M:, to the remote resource. This enables the user to treat the resource as though it was locally connected.

Refer to
Lab Activity
for this chapter

Lab Activity

Map a network drive and share a file.

Summary

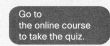

Quiz

Take the chapter quiz to check your knowledge.

Your Chapter Notes

Connecting to the Internet Through an ISP

Introduction

Refer to **Figure** in online course

4.1 The Internet and How We Connect To It

Refer to **Figure** in online course

4.1.1 Explain What the Internet Is

Every day millions of people exchange information through the Internet - but what exactly is the Internet? The Internet is a worldwide collection of computer networks, cooperating with each other to exchange information using common standards. Through telephone wires, fiber optic cables, wireless transmissions and satellite links, Internet users can exchange information in a variety of forms.

The Internet is a network of networks that connects users in every country in the world. There are currently over one billion Internet users worldwide.

Up to now the networks we have discussed have been controlled by one individual or organization. The Internet is a conglomerate of networks and is owned by no one individual or group. There are, however, several major International organizations that help manage the Internet so that everyone uses the same rules.

4.1.2 Internet Service Providers (ISPs)

Refer to **Figure** in online course

Any home, business or organization that wants to connect to the Internet must use an Internet Service Provider (*ISP*). An ISP is a company that provides the connections and support to access the Internet. It can also provide additional services such as Email and *web hosting*.

ISPs are essential to gaining access to the Internet. No one gets on the Internet without a host computer, and no one gets on the Internet without going through an ISP.

ISPs range in size from small to very large and differ in terms of the area they service. ISPs may provide limited services to a small geographical area or can have a wide variety of services and support entire countries with millions of customers. ISPs also differ in the types of connection technologies and speeds they offer. Examples of well known ISPs include AOL, EarthLink, and Roadrunner.

Do you have Internet access? Who is your ISP?

4.1.3 The ISPs Relationship with the Internet

Refer to **Figure** in online course

Individual computers and local networks connect to the ISP at a *Point of Presence* (POP). A POP is the connection point between the ISP's network and the particular geographical region that the POP is servicing.

An ISP may have many POPs depending on its size and the area it services. Within an ISP, a network of high-speed routers and switches move data between the various POPs. Multiple links interconnect the POPs to provide alternate routes for the data should one link fail or become overloaded with traffic and congested.

ISPs connect to other ISPs in order to send information beyond the boundaries of their own network. The Internet is made up of very high-speed data links that interconnect ISP POPs and ISPs to each other. These interconnections are part of the very large, high capacity network known as the Internet Backbone.

Connecting to the ISP at the POP provides users with access to the ISP's services and the Internet.

4.1.4 Options for Connecting to the ISP

Refer to **Figure** in online course

ISPs provide a variety of ways to connect to the Internet, depending on location and desired connection speed.

In a major city there are typically more choices for ISPs and more connection options than in a rural area. For example, cable Internet access is only available in certain metropolitan areas where cable TV service is available. Remote areas may only have access via *dial-up* or satellite.

Each Internet access technology uses a network access device, such as a modem, in order to connect to the ISP. It may be built in to your computer or may be provided by the ISP.

The simplest arrangement is a modem that provides a direct connection between a computer and the ISP. However, if multiple computers connect through a single ISP connection, you will need additional networking devices. This includes a switch to connect multiple hosts on a local network, and a router to move packets from your local network to the ISP network. A home networking device, such as an integrated router, can provide these functions, as well as wireless capability, in a single package.

Refer to **Figure** in online course

The choice of Internet access technologies depends on availability, cost, access device used, media used and the speed of the connection.

Most of the technologies shown are used for both home and small business. Leased lines are typically used for business and large organizations, but can be used to provide high speed connectivity in areas where cable or DSL are not available.

4.1.5 ISP Levels of Service

Refer to **Figure** in online course

Depending on the ISP and the connection technology, various services are available such as *virus* scanning, video on demand, and file storage. The contract with the ISP determines the type and level of services that are available. Most ISPs offer two different contract levels: home service or business class service.

Home service is normally less expensive than business services, and generally provides scaled-down services such as slower connection speed, reduced web space storage, and fewer email accounts. A typical home account may include a minimum of five email addresses with additional addresses being available for a fee.

Business class service is more expensive but provides faster connection speeds and additional web space and email accounts. A business class service may include twenty, fifty or more email addresses. Business service also includes agreements between the ISP and the customer specifying items such as network availability and service response time. These are known as Service Level Agreements (SLAs).

Refer to **Figure** in online course

When data is transferred, it is either uploaded or downloaded. Downloading refers to information coming from the Internet to your computer, while uploading indicates the reverse path, from your computer to the Internet. When the download transfer rate is different from the upload transfer rate, it is called asymmetric. When the transfer rate is the same in both directions, it is called symmetric. ISPs can offer both asymmetric and symmetric services.

Asymmetric:

- Most commonly used for the home.

- Download speeds are faster than upload speeds.

- Necessary for users that download significantly more than upload.

- Most Internet users, especially those who use graphics or multimedia intensive web data, need lots of download bandwidth.

Symmetric:

- Most commonly used for business or individuals hosting servers on the Internet.

- Used when necessary to upload large amounts of traffic such as intensive graphics, multimedia, or video.

- It can carry large amounts of data in both directions at equal rates.

Refer to **Interactive Graphic** in online course.

Activity

Match the requirements of an end-user to various ISPs.

After reading the scenario, place a check in the box of the most appropriate ISP for each user.

4.2 Sending Information Across the Internet

4.2.1 Importance of the Internet Protocol (IP)

Refer to **Figure** in online course

For hosts to communicate on the Internet, they must be running Internet Protocol (IP) software. The IP protocol is one of a group of protocols that are collectively referred to as TCP/IP (Transmission Control Protocol / Internet Protocol). The Internet Protocol (IP) uses packets to carry data. Whether you are playing an Internet video game, chatting with a friend, sending email or searching the Web, the information you are sending or receiving is carried in the form of IP packets.

Each IP packet must contain a valid source and destination IP address. Without valid address information, packets sent will not reach the destination host. Return packets will not make it back to the original source.

IP defines the structure of the source and destination IP addresses. It specifies how these addresses are used in routing of packets from one host or network to another.

All protocols that operate on the Internet, including IP, are defined in numbered standards documents called RFCs (Request for Comments).

Refer to **Figure** in online course

An IP packet has a *header* at the beginning which contains the source and destination IP addresses. It also contains control information that describes the packet to network devices, such as routers, it passes through and also helps to control its behavior on the network. The IP packet is sometimes referred to as a *datagram*.

IP addresses must be unique on the Internet. There are organizations responsible for controlling the distribution of IP addresses so that there is no duplication. ISPs obtain blocks of IP addresses from a local, national or regional Internet registry (RIR). It is the responsibly of the ISPs to manage these addresses and assign them to end users.

Computers in homes, small businesses and other organizations obtain their IP configuration from their ISP. Typically, this configuration is obtained automatically when the user connects to the ISP for Internet access.

4.2.2 How ISPs Handle Packets

Refer to **Figure** in online course

Before being sent on the Internet, messages are divided into packets. IP packet size is between 64 to 1500 bytes for Ethernet networks, and contains mostly user data. Downloading a single 1 MB song would require over 600 packets of 1500 bytes. Each individual packet must have a source and destination IP address.

When a packet is sent across the Internet, the ISP determines whether the packet is destined for a local service located on the ISP network, or a remote service located on a different network.

Every ISP has a control facility for their network, known as the Network Operations Center (*NOC*). The NOC usually controls traffic flow and houses services such as email and web hosting. The NOC may be located at one of the POPs or at a completely separate facility within the ISP network. Packets looking for local services are usually forwarded to the NOC and never leave the ISP network.

Refer to **Figure** in online course

Routers in each of the ISP POPs use the destination address of the IP packets to choose the best path through the Internet. The packets you send to the ISP POP are forwarded by routers through the ISP's network and then through the networks of other ISPs. They pass from router to router until they reach their final destination.

4.2.3 Forwarding Packets Across the Internet

Refer to **Figure** in online course

There are network utilities that test connectivity to the destination device. The `ping` utility tests end-to-end connectivity between source and destination. It measures the time that it takes test packets to make a round trip from the source to the destination and whether the transmission is successful. However, if the packet does not reach the destination, or if delays are encountered along the way, there is no way to determine where the problem is located.

How is it possible to determine which routers the packets have passed through and detect the problem areas in the path?

The `traceroute` utility traces the route from source to destination. Each router through which the packets travel is referred to as a hop. **Traceroute** displays each hop along the way and the time it takes for each one. If a problem occurs, the display of the time and the route that the packet traveled can help to determine where the packet was lost or delayed. The `traceroute` utility is called `tracert` in the Windows environment.

There are also a number of visual `traceroute` programs that can provide a graphical display of the route that a packet takes.

Refer to **Packet Tracer Activity** for this chapter

Packet Tracer Activity

Use `ping` and `traceroute` to check connectivity and learn more about how packets travel through the Internet.

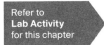

Lab Activity

Use `ping`, `traceroute`, `visual traceroute` and `whois` to check connectivity and IP addresses and learn more about how packets travel through the Internet.

4.3 Networking Devices in a NOC

4.3.1 Internet Cloud

When packets travel across the Internet, they pass through many network devices.

The Internet can be thought of as a network of routers, interconnected with one another. Very often, there are alternate routes between routers, and packets may take different paths between source and destination.

Should there be a problem with traffic flow at any point in the network; packets automatically take an alternate route.

A diagram that shows all network devices and their interconnections would be very complex. Additionally, the final routing path between source and destination is not usually important, only that the source is able to communicate with the destination. Therefore, in network diagrams a *cloud* is often used to represent the Internet or any other complex network, without showing the details of the connections. The cloud allows for simple diagrams that focus on source and destination only, even though there may be many devices linked in-between.

4.3.2 Devices in Internet Cloud

Routers are not the only devices found in the Internet cloud nor are they the only devices found at an ISP. The ISP must be able to accept and deliver information to the end-user as well as participate in the Internet.

Devices that provide connectivity to end-users must match the technology used by the end-user to connect to the ISP. For example, if the end-user is using DSL technology to connect, the ISP must have a DSL Access Multiplexer (*DSLAM*) to accept these connections. For cable modems to connect, the ISP must have a Cable Modem Termination System (*CMTS*). Some ISPs still accept analog calls through modems and have banks of modems to support these users. ISPs that provide wireless access have wireless bridging equipment.

The ISP must also be able to connect with and transfer data with other ISPs. A variety of technologies are used to accomplish this, each requiring specialized equipment and configurations in order to function.

The type of equipment found in an ISP equipment room depends on the technology of the networks in which it is participating. Routers and switches make up most of this equipment. But these devices are very different than the ones found in the home or small business environment.

Networking devices used by the ISP handle extremely large volumes of traffic very quickly. They must function at near 100% uptime since the failure of a key piece of equipment at an ISP can have disastrous effects on network traffic. For this reason, most of the equipment used by ISPs are high-end, high-speed devices with redundancy.

In contrast, network devices used in the home or small business environment are lower-end, lower-speed devices that are not capable of handling large volumes of traffic. Integrated routers can perform several functions, including: Wireless LAN access point, switching, routing, firewalls and various address functions. An integrated router may support some or all of these functions.

Refer to
Interactive Graphic
in online course.

Activity

Amelia has been hired as a Network Support Analyst for a major ISP. On her first day, she will be going on a tour of the NOC's equipment room.

Amelia is expecting to see certain equipment and features present in the room. She has started to compile a list of these features.

Complete the table by explaining reasons why the listed features are critical to the room.

4.3.3 Physical and Environmental Requirements

Refer to
Figure
in online course

The network installation located at an ISP versus a home/small business are very different.

The home or small business network provides a limited number of services for relatively few users. Internet connectivity is purchased from an ISP. The volume of traffic is small, and no transport services are provided.

The ISP provides transport and other services to a large number of users. A number of different devices are required to accept input from end users. To participate in a transport network, they must be able to connect to other ISPs. They handle large volumes of traffic and require very reliable equipment in order to handle the load.

Even though these two networks appear very different, they both require an environment where the equipment can function reliably and without interruption. The requirements are the same, but the scale of operation is different: at home, a single power outlet will suffice, whereas at an ISP the power requirements need to be planned out ahead of time and installed.

Refer to
Figure
in online course

One major difference between an ISP and a home/small business network is the inclusion of servers. Most home users do not run servers and small businesses usually may have a few. They rely on the services offered by the ISP for such things as email, address assignment and web space. An ISP must consider the physical requirements of not only the networking equipment, but also the servers it houses.

One of the main considerations for electronic equipment is a reliable supply of stable power. Unfortunately the supply of power is not always reliable, and this can lead to problems for network devices. ISPs install power conditioning equipment with substantial battery backup to maintain *continuity* of supply should the main power grid fail. For the home/small business, inexpensive uninterruptible power supplies (UPS) and battery backup units are usually sufficient for the relatively small amount of equipment they use.

Refer to
Figure
in online course

Environmental factors, such as heat and humidity, must also be considered when planning a network installation. However, because of the volume of equipment and the amount of power consumed in an ISP, high-end air conditioning units are necessary to maintain controlled temperatures. For the home/small business, ordinary air conditioning, heating, and humidity controls are usually sufficient.

Cable management is another area of concern for both the home/small business network and the ISP. Cables must be protected from physical damage and organized in a manner that will aid in the troubleshooting process. In small networks, there are only a few cables, but in ISP networks, thousands of cables must be managed. This can include not only copper data cables but also fiber optic and power cables.

All of these factors, namely power supply, environment and cable management, must be considered when setting up a network of any size. There is a big variation between size and therefore requirements for an ISP and a home network. Most networks fall somewhere between these two extremes.

4.4 Cables and Connectors

4.4.1 Common Network Cables

Refer to
Figure
in online course

In order for communication to occur a source, destination, and some sort of channel must be present. A channel, or medium, provides a path over which the information is sent. In the networked world, the medium is usually some sort of physical cable. It may also be electromagnetic radiation, in the case of wireless networking. The connection between the source and destination may either be direct or indirect, and may span multiple media types.

Many different types of cables exist to interconnect the various devices in a NOC or local network.

There are two kinds of physical cable. Metal cables, usually copper, have electrical impulses applied to them to convey information. Fiber optic cables, made of glass or plastic, use flashes of light to convey information.

Refer to
Figure
in online course

Twisted Pair

Modern Ethernet technology generally uses a type of copper cable known as twisted pair (TP) to interconnect devices. Because Ethernet is the foundation for most local networks, TP is the most commonly encountered type of network cabling.

Coaxial Cable

Coaxial cable is usually constructed of either copper or aluminum, and is used by cable television companies to provide service. It is also used for connecting the various components which make up satellite communication systems.

Fiber Optic

Fiber optic cables are made of glass or plastic. They have a very high bandwidth, which enables them to carry very large amounts of data. Fiber is used in backbone networks, large enterprise environments and large data centers. It is also used extensively by telephone companies.

4.4.2 Twisted Pair Cables

Refer to
Figure
in online course

Twisted pair cables consist of one or more pairs of insulated copper wires that are twisted together and housed in a protective jacket. Like all copper cables, twisted pair uses pulses of electricity to transmit data.

Data transmission is sensitive to interference or noise, which can reduce the data rate that a cable can provide. A twisted pair cable is susceptible to electromagnetic interference (*EMI*), a type of noise.

A source of interference, known as crosstalk, occurs when cables are bundled together for long lengths. The signal from one cable can leak out and enter adjacent cables.

When data transmission is corrupted due to interference such as crosstalk, the data must be retransmitted. This can degrade the data carrying capacity of the medium.

In twisted pair cabling, the number of twists per unit length affects the amount of resistance that the cable has to interference. Twisted pair cable suitable for carrying telephone traffic, referred to as CAT3, has 3-4 turns per foot making it less resistant. Cable suitable for data transmission, known as CAT5, has 3-4 turns per inch, making it more resistant to interference.

Refer to
Figure
in online course

There are three types of twisted pair cable: unshielded twisted pair, shielded twisted pair, and screened twisted pair.

Unshielded twisted pair (UTP) is the most commonly encountered type of network cable in North America and many other areas. Shielded cables (ScTP and F-UTP) are used almost exclusively in European countries.

UTP cable is inexpensive, offers a high bandwidth, and is easy to install. This type of cable is used to connect workstations, hosts and network devices. It can come with many different numbers of pairs inside the jacket, but the most common number of pairs is four. Each pair is identified by a specific color code.

Many different categories of UTP cables have been developed over time. Each category of cable was developed to support a specific technology and most are no longer encountered in homes or offices. The cable types which are still commonly found include Categories 3, 5, 5e and 6. There are electrical environments in which EMI and *RFI* are so strong that shielding is a requirement to make communication possible, such as in a noisy factory. In this instance, it may be necessary to use a cable that contains shielding, such as Shielded twisted-pair (STP) and Screened twisted-pair (ScTP). Unfortunately both STP and ScTP are very expensive, not as flexible, and have additional requirements due to the shielding that make them difficult to work with.

All Categories of data grade UTP cable are traditionally terminated into an RJ-45 connector.

4.4.3 Coaxial Cable

Refer to **Figure** in online course

Like twisted pair, coaxial cable (or coax) also carries data in the form of electrical signals. It provides improved shielding compared to UTP, so has a lower signal-to-noise ratio and can therefore carry more data. It is often used to connect a TV set to the signal source, be it a cable TV outlet, satellite TV, or conventional antenna. It is also used at NOCs to connect to the cable modem termination system (CMTS) and to connect to some high-speed interfaces.

Although coax has improved data carrying characteristics, twisted pair cabling has replaced coax in local area networking uses. Among the reasons for the replacement is that - compared to UTP - coax is physically harder to install, more expensive, and harder to troubleshoot.

4.4.4 Fiber Optic Cables

Refer to **Figure** in online course

Unlike TP and coax, fiber optic cables transmit data using pulses of light. Although not normally found in home or small business environments, fiber optic cabling is widely used in enterprise environments and large data centers.

Fiber optic cable is constructed of either glass or plastic, neither of which conducts electricity. This means that it is immune to EMI and is suitable for installation in environments where interference is a problem.

In addition to its resistance to EMI, fiber optic cables support a large amount of bandwidth making them ideally suited for high-speed data backbones. Fiber optic backbones are found in many corporations and are also used to connect ISPs on the Internet.

Each fiber optic circuit is actually two fiber cables. One is used to transmit data; the other is used to receive data.

Refer to **Figure** in online course

There are two forms of fiber optic cable: multimode and single mode.

Multimode

Of the two forms of fiber optic, multimode is the less expensive and more widely used. The light source that produces the pulses of light is usually an *LED*. It is referred to as multimode because there are multiple rays of light, each carrying data, being transmitted through the cable simultaneously. Each ray of light takes a separate path through the multimode core. Multimode fiber optical cables are generally suitable for links of up to 2000 meters. However, improvements in technology are continually improving this distance.

Single Mode

Single mode fiber optic cables are constructed in such a way that light can follow only a single path through the fiber. The light source for single mode fiber optic cables is usually a LED laser, which is significantly more expensive and intense than ordinary LEDs. Due to the intensity of the LED laser, much higher data rates and longer ranges can be obtained. Single mode fibers can transmit data for approximately 3000 meters and are used for backbone cabling including the interconnection of various NOCs. Again, improvements in technology are continually improving this distance.

Refer to
Interactive Graphic
in online course.

Activity

Decide if copper or fiber is the best solution to a cabling requirement.

Check either copper or fiber optic next to the description.

4.5 Working with Twisted Pair Cabling

4.5.1 Cabling Standards

Refer to
Figure
in online course

Cabling is an integral part of building any network. When installing cable, it is important to follow cabling standards, which have been developed to ensure data networks operate to agreed levels of performance.

Cabling standards are a set of specifications for the installation and testing of cables. Standards specify types of cables to use in specific environments, conductor materials, pinouts, wire sizes, shielding, cable lengths, connector types and performance limits.

There are many different organizations involved in the creation of cabling standards. While some of these organizations have only local jurisdiction many offer standards that are adopted around the world.

Some of the organizations and the areas that they manage are seen in the graphic.

4.5.2 UTP Cables

Refer to
Figure
in online course

Twisted pair cable is most commonly used in network installations. The TIA/EIA organization defines two different patterns, or wiring schemes, called T568A and T568B. Each wiring scheme defines the pinout, or order of wire connections, on the end of the cable.

The two schemes are similar except two of the four pairs are reversed in the termination order. The graphic shows this color-coding and how the two pairs are reversed.

On a network installation, one of the two wiring schemes (T568A or T568B) should be chosen and followed. It is important that the same wiring scheme is used for every termination in that project. If working on an existing network, use the wiring scheme already employed.

Refer to
Figure
in online course

Using the T568A and T568B wiring schemes, two types of cables can be created: a straight-through cable and a crossover cable. These two types of cable are found in data installations.

Straight-through Cables

A Straight-through cable is the most common cable type. It maps a wire to the same pins on both ends of the cable. In other words, if T568A is on one end of the cable, T568A is also on the other.

If T568B is on one end of the cable, T568B is on the other. This means that the order of connections (the pinout) for each color is the exact same on both ends.

It is the type of straight-through cable (T568A or T568B) used on the network that defines the wiring scheme for the network.

Crossover Cable

A crossover cable uses both wiring schemes. T568A on one end of the cable and T568B on the other end of the same cable. This means that the order of connection on one end of the cable does not match the order of connections on the other.

The straight-through and crossover cables each have a specific use on the network. The type of cable needed to connect two devices depends on which wire pairs the devices use to transmit and receive data.

Refer to
Figure
in online course

Specific pins on the connector are associated with a transmit function and a receive function. The transmit pin versus the receive pin is determined based on the device.

Two devices directly connected and using different pins for transmit and receive are known as unlike devices. They require a straight-through cable to exchange data. Devices that are directly connected and use the same pins for transmit and receive, are known as like devices. They require the use of a crossover cable to exchange data.

Unlike Devices

The pins on the RJ-45 data connector of a PC have pins 1 and 2 as transmit and pins 3 and 6 as receive. The pins on the data connector of a switch have pins 1 and 2 as receive and pins 3 and 6 as transmit. The pins used for transmit on the PC correspond to those used for receive on the switch. Therefore, a straight-through cable is necessary.

The wire connected to pin 1 (transmit pin) on the PC on one end of the cable, is connected to pin 1 (receive pin) on the switch on the other end of the cable.

Other examples of unlike devices that require a straight-through cable include:

- Switch port to router port
- Hub port to PC

Refer to
Figure
in online course

Like Devices

If a PC is directly connected to another PC, pins 1 and 2 on both devices are transmit pins and pins 3 and 6 are receive pins.

A crossover cable would ensure that the green wire connected to pins 1 and 2 (transmit pins) on one PC connect to pins 3 and 6 (receive pins) on the other PC.

If a straight-through cable were used, the wire connected to pin 1, the transmit pin, on PC1 would be connected to pin 1, the transmit pin, on PC2. It is not possible to receive data on a transmit pin.

Other examples of like devices that require a crossover cable include:

- Switch port to switch port
- Switch port to hub port
- Hub port to hub port
- Router port to router port
- PC to router port

■ PC to PC

If the incorrect cable type is used, the connection between network devices will not function.

Some devices can automatically sense which pins are used for transmit and receive and will adjust their internal connections accordingly.

4.5.3 UTP Cable Termination

Refer to
Figure
in online course

UTP and STP cable is usually terminated into an RJ-45 connector.

The RJ-45 connector is considered a male component, which is crimped to the end of the cable. When a male connector is viewed from the front with the metal contacts facing up, the pin locations are numbered from 8 on the left to 1 on the right.

The jack is considered the female component and is located in networking devices, wall outlets, or patch panels. The RJ-45 connector on the wire plugs into the jack.

Cables can be purchased that are pre-terminated with RJ-45 connectors. They can also be manually terminated, onsite, using a crimping tool. When manually terminating UTP cable into an RJ-45 connector, untwist only a small amount of wire to minimize crosstalk. Also be sure that the wires are pushed all the way into the end of the connector and that the RJ-45 connector is crimped onto the wire jacket. This ensures good electrical contact and provides strength to the wire connection.

Refer to
Lab Activity
for this chapter

Lab Activity

Construct both straight-through and crossover UTP cables.

4.5.4 Terminating UTP at Patch Panels and Wall Jacks

Refer to
Figure
in online course

In a NOC, network devices are usually connected to patch panels. Patch panels act like switchboards that connect workstation cables to other devices. The use of patch panels enables the physical cabling of the network to be quickly rearranged as equipment is added or replaced. These patch panels use RJ-45 jacks for quick connection on the front, but require the cables to be punched down on the reverse side of the RJ-45 jack.

Patch panels are no longer confined to enterprise network installations. They can be found in many small businesses and even homes where they provide a central connection point for data, telephone and even audio systems.

Refer to
Figure
in online course

The RJ-45 jack has eight conductors, and is wired according to either T568A or T568B. At the *patch panel* a device known as a punchdown tool is required to push the wires into the connector. The wires should be matched up to the appropriate insulation displacement connector (IDC) by color before punching them down. The punchdown tool also cuts off any excess wire.

A punchdown tool is not required to terminate most wall jacks. To terminate these connectors the cables are untwisted and placed into the appropriate IDC. Placing the cap on the jack pushes the cables into the IDC and cuts through the insulation on the wires. Most of these connectors then require the installer to manually trim away excess cable.

Refer to
Figure
in online course

In all cases, untwisting more cable than is necessary will increase the amount of crosstalk and degrade overall network performance.

Observe the correct procedure for punching down UTP cable and terminating RJ-45 wall jacks.

Refer to
Lab Activity
for this chapter

Click Play to start the video.

Lab Activity

Use a *punch down tool* to terminate a UTP cable into an IDC and terminate UTP cable into an RJ-45 jack.

4.5.5 Cable Testing

Refer to
Figure
in online course

When a new or repaired cable run is terminated, it is important to verify that the cable operates correctly and meets connectivity standards. This can be done through a series of tests.

The first test is a visual inspection, which verifies that all wires are connected according to T568A or B.

In addition to visual examination, check the cable electrically in order to determine problems or flaws in a network cabling installation. The following are tools that can be used for cable diagnostics:

- Cable testers
- Cable certifiers
- Multimeters

Refer to
Figure
in online course

The cable tester is used to perform initial diagnostics. The first test usually is called a continuity test and it verifies that there is end-to-end connectivity. It can also detect common cabling faults such as opens and *shorts*.

An open circuit occurs when the wire is not properly pushed into the connector and there is no electrical contact. An open can also occur if there is a break in the wire.

A short occurs when the copper conductors touch each other. As the electric pulse travels down the wire, it will cross onto the touching wire. This creates an unintended path in the flow of the signal to its destination.

A cable tester can also create wire maps that will verify that the cable is terminated correctly. A wire map shows which wire pairs connect to which pins on the plugs and sockets. The wire map test verifies that all eight wires are connected to the correct pins and indicates if cabling faults are present such as split pairs or reversals.

If any of these faults are detected, the easiest way to correct them is to reterminate the cable.

Refer to
Figure
in online course

Specialized cable testers provide additional information, such as the level of *attenuation* and crosstalk.

Attenuation

Attenuation, also commonly referred to as insertion loss, is a general term that refers to the reduction in the strength of a signal. Attenuation is a natural consequence of signal transmission over any medium. Attenuation limits the length of network cabling over which a message can be sent. For example, Ethernet cable has a distance limitation of 328 feet (100 meters) where as some types of fiber optic cable have a distance limitation of several miles (kilometers). A cable tester measures attenuation by injecting a signal in one end and then measuring its strength at the other end.

Crosstalk

Crosstalk is the leakage of signals between pairs. If this is measured near the transmitting end it is termed near-end crosstalk (*NEXT*). If measured at the receiving end of the cable it is termed far-end crosstalk (*FEXT*). Both forms of crosstalk degrade network performance and are often caused by untwisting too much cable when terminating. If high crosstalk values are detected, the best thing to do is check the cable terminations and re-terminate as necessary.

Refer to
Lab Activity
for this chapter

Lab Activity

Test the cable created in a previous lab session.

4.5.6 Cabling Best Practices

Refer to
Figure
in online course

The following steps, called best practices, ensure that cable termination is successful.

1. It is important that the type of cables and components used on a network adhere to the standards required for that network. Modern converged networks carry voice, video and data traffic on the same wires; therefore the cables used on converged networks must be able to support all these applications.

2. Cable standards specify maximum lengths for different types of cables. Always adhere to the length restrictions for the type of cable being installed.

3. UTP, like all copper cable, is susceptible to EMI. It is important to install cable away from sources of interference such as high-voltage cables and fluorescent lighting. Televisions, computer monitors and microwaves are other possible sources of interference. In some environments it may be necessary to install data cables in conduit to protect them from EMI and RFI.

4. Improper termination and the use of low quality cables and connectors can degrade the signal carrying capacity of the cable. Always follow the rules for cable termination and test to verify that the termination has been done properly.

5. Test all cable installations to ensure proper connectivity and operation.

6. Label all cables as they are installed, and record the location of cables in network documentation.

Refer to
Figure
in online course

Structured cabling is a method for creating an organized cabling system that can be easily understood by installers, network administrators, and any other technicians who deal with cables. One component of structured cabling is cable management.

Cable management serves multiple purposes. First, it presents a neat and organized system which aids in the isolation of cabling problems. Second, by following cable management best practices, the cables are protected from physical damage which greatly reduces the number of problems experienced.

Cables should be considered a long term investment. What may be sufficient now may not be in the near future. Always plan for the future by complying with all current standards. Remember that standards help to ensure that the cables will be able to deliver acceptable performance as the technology evolves.

It is important to observe cabling best practices in all environments. Strict adherence to these practices, in home and business environments, helps reduce the number of potential problems. It will save a great amount of time, money and frustration.

Refer to
Interactive Graphic
in online course.

Activity

Decide if an operation is a cabling best practice or not.

Check Yes if the statement describes a best practice or No if it does not.

Summary

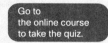

Go to
the online course
to take the quiz.

Quiz

Take the chapter quiz to check your knowledge.

Your Chapter Notes

CHAPTER 5

Network Addressing

Introduction

Refer to
Figure
in online course

5.1 IP Addresses and Subnet Masks

5.1.1 Purpose of the IP Address

Refer to
Figure
in online course

A host needs an IP address to participate on the Internet. The IP address is a logical network address that identifies a particular host. It must be properly configured and unique in order to communicate with other devices on the Internet.

An IP address is assigned to the Network interface connection for a host. This connection is usually a network interface card (NIC) installed in the device. Examples of end-user devices with network interfaces include workstations, servers, network printers and IP phones. Some servers can have more than one NIC and each of these has its own IP address. Router interfaces that provide connections to an IP network will also have an IP address.

Every packet sent across the Internet has a source and destination IP address. This information is required by networking devices to insure the information gets to the destination and any replies are returned to the source.

Refer to **Packet
Tracer Activity**
for this chapter

Packet Tracer Activity

Use Packet Tracer to ping different websites.

5.1.2 IP Address Structure

Refer to
Figure
in online course

An IP address is simply a series of 32 binary bits (ones and zeros). It is very difficult for humans to read a binary IP address. For this reason, the 32 bits are grouped into four 8-bit bytes called octets. An IP address in this format is hard for humans to read, write and remember. To make the IP address easier to understand, each octet is presented as its decimal value, separated by a decimal point or period. This is referred to as dotted-decimal notation.

When a host is configured with an IP address, it is entered as a dotted decimal number such as 192.168.1.5. Imagine if you had to enter the 32-bit binary equivalent of this-11000000101010000000000100000101. If just one bit was mistyped, the address would be different and the host may not be able to communicate on the network.

The 32-bit IP address is defined with IP version 4 (*IPv4*) and is currently the most common form of IP address on the Internet. There are over 4 billion possible IP addresses using a 32-bit addressing scheme.

Refer to
Figure
in online course

When a host receives an IP address, it looks at all 32 bits as they are received by the NIC. Humans, on the other hand, need to convert those 32 bits into their four *octet* decimal equivalent. Each octet is made up of 8 bits and each bit has a value. The four groups of 8 bits have the same set of values. The rightmost bit in an octet has a value of 1 and the values of the remaining bits, from right to left, are 2, 4, 8, 16, 32, 64 and 128.

Determine the value of the octet by adding the values of positions wherever there is a binary 1 present.

- If there is a 0 in a position, do not add the value.

- If all 8 bits are 0s. 00000000 the value of the octet is 0.

- If all 8 bits are 1s, 11111111 the value of the octet is 255 (128+64+32+16+8+4+2+1).

- If the 8 bits are mixed, such as the example 00100111, the value of the octet is 39 (32+4+2+1).

So the value of each of the four octets can range from 0 to a maximum of 255.

Refer to
Interactive Graphic
in online course.

Activity

Enter binary or dotted decimal IP addresses and convert them. You can also generate IP addresses to test your knowledge.

Enter a binary or dotted decimal address and click "Convert" or click "Test Me" to generate a binary or decimal number and enter your answer.

5.1.3 Parts of an IP Address

Refer to
Figure
in online course

The logical 32-bit IP address is hierarchical and is made up of two parts. The first part identifies the network and the second part identifies a host on that network. Both parts are required in an IP address.

As an example, if a host has IP address 192.168.18.57 the first three octets, (192.168.18), identify the network portion of the address, and the last octet, (57) identifies the host. This is known as hierarchical addressing because the network portion indicates the network on which each unique host address is located. Routers only need to know how to reach each network, rather than needing to know the location of each individual host.

Another example of a hierarchical network is the telephone system. With a telephone number, the country code, area code and exchange represent the network address and the remaining digits represent a local phone number.

Refer to
Interactive Graphic
in online course.

Activity

Drag hosts to the correct network based on network portion of IP address.

Drag each host to the correct network.

5.1.4 How IP Addresses and Subnet Masks Interact

Refer to
Figure
in online course

There are two parts to every IP address. How do hosts know which portion is the network and which is the host? This is the job of the *subnet mask*.

When an IP host is configured, a subnet mask is assigned along with an IP address. Like the IP address, the subnet mask is 32 bits long. The subnet mask signifies which part of the IP address is network and which part is host.

The subnet mask is compared to the IP address from left to right, bit for bit. The 1s in the subnet mask represent the network portion; the 0s represent the host portion. In the example shown, the first three octets are network, and the last octet represents the host.

When a host sends a packet, it compares its subnet mask to its own IP address and the destination IP address. If the network bits match, both the source and destination host are on the same network and the packet can be delivered locally. If they do not match, the sending host forwards the packet to the local router interface to be sent on to the other network.

Refer to **Figure** in online course

The subnet masks we see most often with home and small business networking are: 255.0.0.0 (8-bits), 255.255.0.0 (16 bits) and 255.255.255.0 (24 bits). A subnet mask of 255.255.255.0 (decimal) or 11111111.11111111.1111111.00000000 (binary) uses 24 bits to identify the network number which leaves 8 bits to number the hosts on that network.

To calculate the number of hosts that can be on that network, take the number 2 to the power of the number of host bits (2 ^ 8 = 256). From this number, we must subtract 2 (256-2). The reason we subtract 2 is because all 1s within the host portion of an IP address is a broadcast address for that network and cannot be assigned to a specific host. All 0s within the host portion indicates the network ID and again, cannot be assigned to a specific host. Powers of 2 can be calculated easily with the calculator that comes with any Windows operating system.

Another way to determine the number of hosts available is to add up the values of the available host bits (128+64+32+16+8+4+2+1 = 255). From this number, subtract 1 (255-1 = 254), because the host bits cannot be all 1s. It is not necessary to subtract 2 because the value of all 0s is 0 and is not included in the addition.

With a 16-bit mask, there are 16 bits (two octets) for host addresses and a host address could have all 1s (255) in one of the octets. This might appear to be a broadcast but as long as the other octet is not all 1s, it is a valid host address. Remember that the host looks at all host bits together, not at octet values.

Refer to **Lab Activity** for this chapter

Lab Activity

Convert between binary and decimal numbers. Work with powers of 2 to calculate the number of hosts available with x number of bits in the host portion of the address.

5.2 Types of IP Addresses

5.2.1 IP Address Classes and Default Subnet Masks

Refer to **Figure** in online course

The IP address and subnet mask work together to determine which portion of the IP address represents the network address and which portion represents the host address.

IP addresses are grouped into 5 classes. Classes A, B and C are commercial addresses and are assigned to hosts. *Class D* is reserved for multicast use and *Class E* is for experimental use.

Class C addresses have three octets for the network portion and one for the hosts. The default subnet mask is 24 bits (255.255.255.0). Class C addresses are usually assigned to small networks.

Class B addresses have two octets to represent the network portion and two for the hosts. The default subnet mask is 16 bits (255.255.0.0). These addresses are typically used for medium-sized networks.

Class A addresses have only one octet to represent the network portion and three to represent the hosts. The default subnet mask is 8 bits (255.0.0.0). These addresses are typically assigned to large organizations.

The class of an address can be determined by the value of the first octet. For instance, if the first octet of an IP address has a value in the range 192-223, it is classified as a Class C address. As an example, 200.14.193.67 is a Class C address.

Refer to
Interactive Graphic
in online course.

Activity

Click the proper subnet mask to stop the IP addresses from falling and score points.

Click the subnet mask to begin.

5.2.2 Public and Private IP Addresses

Refer to
Figure
in online course

All hosts that connect directly to the Internet require a unique *public IP address*. Because of the finite number of 32-bit addresses available, there is a risk of running out of IP addresses. One solution to this problem was to reserve some private addresses for use exclusively inside an organization. This allows hosts within an organization to communicate with one another without the need of a unique public IP address.

RFC 1918 is a standard that reserves several ranges of addresses within each of the classes A, B and C. As shown in the table, these private address ranges consist of a single Class A network, 16 Class B networks and 256 Class C networks. This gives a network administrator considerable flexibility in assigning internal addresses.

A very large network can use the Class A private network, which allows for over 16 million private addresses.

On medium size networks, a Class B private network could be used, which provides over 65,000 addresses.

Home and small business networks typically use a single class C private address, which allows up to 254 hosts.

The Class A network, the 16 Class B networks, or the 256 Class C networks can be used within any size organization. Typically many organizations use the Class A private network.

Refer to
Figure
in online course

Private addresses can be used internally by hosts in an organization as long as the hosts do not connect directly to the Internet. Therefore, the same set of private addresses can be used by multiple organizations. Private addresses are not routed on the Internet and will be quickly blocked by an ISP router.

The use of private addresses can provide a measure of security since they are only visible on the local network, and outsiders cannot gain direct access to the private IP addresses.

There are also private addresses that can be used for the diagnostic testing of devices. This type of private address is known as a loopback address. The class A, 127.0.0.0 network, is reserved for loopback addresses.

Refer to
Interactive Graphic
in online course.

Activity

Drag the IP addresses and drop them into the correct category, either "Public" (the Internet) or "Private" area (small local net).

Drag each IP address to the correct category.

5.2.3 Unicast, Broadcast and Multicast Addresses

Refer to
Figure
in online course

In addition to address classes, we also categorize IP addresses as unicast, broadcast, or multicast. Hosts can use IP addresses to communicate one-to-one (unicast), one-to-many (multicast) or one-to-all (broadcast).

Unicast

A unicast address is the most common type on an IP network. A packet with a unicast destination address is intended for a specific host. An example is a host with IP address 192.168.1.5 (source) requesting a web page from a server at IP address 192.168.1.200 (destination).

For a unicast packet to be sent and received, a destination IP address must be in the IP packet header. A corresponding destination MAC address must also be present in the Ethernet frame header. The IP address and MAC address combine to deliver data to one specific destination host.

Refer to
Figure
in online course

Broadcast

With a broadcast, the packet contains a destination IP address with all ones (1s) in the host portion. This means that all hosts on that local network (broadcast domain) will receive and look at the packet. Many network protocols, such as ARP and *DHCP* use broadcasts.

A Class C network 192.168.1.0 with a default subnet mask of 255.255.255.0 has a broadcast address of 192.168.1.255. The host portion is decimal 255 or binary 11111111 (all 1s).

A Class B network of 172.16.0.0, with a default mask of 255.255.0.0, has a broadcast of 172.16.255.255.

A Class A network of 10.0.0.0, with a default mask of 255.0.0.0, has a broadcast of 10.255.255.255..

A broadcast IP address for a network needs a corresponding broadcast MAC address in the Ethernet frame. On Ethernet networks, the broadcast MAC address is 48 ones displayed as Hexadecimal FF-FF-FF-FF-FF-FF.

Refer to
Figure
in online course

Multicast

Multicast addresses allow a source device to send a packet to a group of devices.

Devices that belong to a multicast group are assigned a multicast group IP address. The range of multicast addresses is from 224.0.0.0 to 239.255.255.255. Since multicast addresses represent a group of addresses (sometimes called a host group), they can only be used as the destination of a packet. The source will always have a unicast address.

Examples of where multicast addresses would be used are in remote gaming, where many players are connected remotely but playing the same game. Another example would be distance learning through video conferencing, where many students are connected to the same class.

As with a unicast or broadcast address, multicast IP addresses need a corresponding multicast MAC address to actually deliver frames on a local network. The multicast MAC address is a special value that begins with 01-00-5E in hexadecimal. The value ends by converting the lower 23 bits of the IP multicast group address into the remaining 6 hexadecimal characters of the Ethernet address. An example, as shown in the graphic, is hexadecimal 01-00-5E-0F-64-C5. Each hexadecimal character is 4 binary bits.

Refer to
Interactive Graphic
in online course.

Activity

Click the host(s) that will receive a packet based on the address type (Unicast, Broadcast or Multicast).

5.3 How IP Addresses are Obtained

5.3.1 Static and Dynamic Address Assignment

Refer to
Figure
in online course

IP addresses can be assigned either statically or dynamically.

Static

With a static assignment, the network administrator must manually configure the network information for a host. At a minimum, this includes the host IP address, subnet mask and default gateway.

Static addresses have some advantages. For instance, they are useful for printers, servers and other networking devices that need to be accessible to clients on the network. If hosts normally access a server at a particular IP address, it would not be good if that address changed.

Static assignment of addressing information can provide increased control of network resources, but it can be time consuming to enter the information on each host. When entering IP addresses statically, the host only performs basic error checks on the IP address. Therefore, errors are more likely to occur.

When using static IP addressing, it is important to maintain an accurate list of which IP addresses are assigned to which devices. Additionally, these are permanent addresses and are not normally reused.

Refer to
Figure
in online course

Dynamic

On local networks it is often the case that the user population changes frequently. New users arrive with laptops and need a connection. Others have new workstations that need to be connected. Rather than have the network administrator assign IP addresses for each workstation, it is easier to have IP addresses assigned automatically. This is done using a protocol known as Dynamic Host Configuration Protocol (DHCP).

DHCP provides a mechanism for the automatic assignment of addressing information such as IP address, subnet mask, default gateway, and other configuration information.

DHCP is generally the preferred method of assigning IP addresses to hosts on large networks since it reduces the burden on network support staff and virtually eliminates entry errors.

Another benefit of DHCP is that an address is not permanently assigned to a host but is only leased for a period of time. If the host is powered down or taken off the network, the address is returned to the pool for reuse. This is especially helpful with mobile users that come and go on a network.

5.3.2 DHCP Servers

Refer to
Figure
in online course

If you enter a wireless hotspot at an airport or coffee shop, DHCP makes it possible for you to access the Internet. As you enter the area, your laptop DHCP client contacts the local *DHCP server* via a wireless connection. The DHCP server assigns an IP address to your laptop.

Various types of devices can be DHCP servers as long as they are running DHCP service software. With most medium to large networks, the DHCP server is usually a local dedicated PC-based server.

With home networks the DHCP server is usually located at the ISP and a host on the home network receives its IP configuration directly from the ISP.

Many home networks and small businesses use an integrated router to connect to the ISP modem. In this case, the integrated router is both a DHCP client and a server. The integrated router acts as a client to receive its IP configuration from the ISP and then acts a DHCP server for internal hosts on the local network.

In addition to PC-based servers and integrated routers, other types of networking devices such as dedicated routers can provide DHCP services to clients, although this is not as common.

5.3.3 Configuring DHCP

Refer to **Figure** in online course

When a host is first configured as a DHCP client, it does not have an IP address, subnet mask or default gateway. It obtains this information from a DHCP server, either on the local network or one located at the ISP. The DHCP server is configured with a range, or pool, of IP addresses that can be assigned to DHCP clients.

A client that needs an IP address will send a DHCP Discover message which is a broadcast with a destination IP address of 255.255.255.255 (32 ones) and a destination MAC address of FF-FF-FF-FF-FF-FF (48 ones). All hosts on the network will receive this broadcast DHCP frame, but only a DHCP server will reply. The server will respond with a DHCP Offer, suggesting an IP address for the client. The host then sends a DHCP Request to that server asking to use the suggested IP address. The server responds with a DHCP Acknowledgment.

Refer to **Figure** in online course

For most home and small business networks, a multi-function device provides DHCP services to the local network clients. To configure a Linksys wireless router, access its graphical web interface by opening the browser and entering the in the Address area the router default IP address: 192.168.1.1. Navigate to the screen that shows the DHCP configuration.

The IP address of 192.168.1.1 and subnet mask of 255.255.255.0 are the defaults for the internal router interface. This is the default gateway for all hosts on the local network and also the internal DHCP server IP address. Most Linksys wireless routers and other home integrated routers have DHCP Server enabled by default.

On the DHCP configuration screen a default *DHCP range* is available or you can specify a starting address for the DHCP range (do not use 192.168.1.1) and the number of addresses to be assigned. The lease time can also be modified (default is 24 hours). The DHCP configuration feature on most ISRs gives information about connected hosts and IP addresses, their associated MAC address, and lease times.

The DHCP Client Table also shows the client name and whether it is connected via the Ethernet LAN or wireless (Interface).

Refer to **Packet Tracer Activity** for this chapter

Packet Tracer Activity

Configure a device as a DHCP server and specify a range of IP addresses. Configure a DHCP client and verify the DHCP configurations.

5.4 Address Management

5.4.1 Network Boundaries and Address Space

Refer to **Figure** in online course

The router provides a gateway through which hosts on one network can communicate with hosts on different networks. Each interface on a router is connected to a separate network.

The IP address assigned to the interface identifies which local network is connected directly to it.

Every host on a network must use the router as a gateway to other networks. Therefore, each host must know the IP address of the router interface connected to the network where the host is attached. This address is known as the default gateway address. It can be either statically configured on the host, or received dynamically by DHCP.

When an integrated router is configured to be a DHCP server for the local network, it automatically sends the correct interface IP address to the hosts as the default gateway address. In this manner, all hosts on the network can use that IP address to forward messages to hosts located at the

ISP and get access to hosts on the Internet. Integrated routers are usually set to be DHCP servers by default.

The IP address of that local router interface becomes the default gateway address for the host configuration. The default gateway is provided, either statically or by DHCP.

When an integrated router is configured as a DHCP server, it provides its own internal IP address as the default gateway to DHCP clients. It also provides them with their respective IP address and subnet mask.

5.4.2 Address Assignment

Refer to
Figure
in online course

The integrated router acts as a DHCP server for all local hosts attached to it, either by Ethernet cable or wirelessly. These local hosts are referred to as being located on an internal, or inside, network. Most DHCP servers are configured to assign private addresses to the hosts on the internal network, rather than Internet routable public addresses. This ensures that, by default, the internal network is not directly accessible from the Internet.

The default IP address configured on the local integrated router interface is usually a private Class C address. Internal hosts must be assigned addresses within the same network as the integrated router, either statically configured, or through DHCP. When configured as a DHCP server, the integrated router provides addresses in this range. It also provides the subnet mask information and its own interface IP address as the default gateway.

Many ISPs also use DHCP servers to provide IP addresses to the Internet side of the integrated router installed at their customer sites. The network assigned to the Internet side of the integrated router is referred to as the external, or outside, network.

When an integrated router is connected to the ISP, it acts like a DHCP client to receive the correct external network IP address for the Internet interface. ISPs usually provide an Internet-routable address, which enables hosts connected to the integrated router to have access to the Internet.

The integrated router serves as the boundary between the local internal network and the external Internet.

Refer to
Figure
in online course

There are several ways hosts can be connected to an ISP and the Internet. Whether or not an individual host is assigned a public or private address depends on how it is connected.

Direct Connection

Some customers have just a single computer with a direct connection from the ISP through a modem. In this case, the public address from the ISP DHCP server is assigned to the single host.

Connection Through an Integrated Router

When there is more than one host that needs access to the Internet, the ISP modem can be attached directly to an integrated router instead of directly to a single computer. This enables the creation of a home or small business network. The integrated router receives the public address from the ISP. Internal hosts receive private addresses from the integrated router.

Connection Through a Gateway Device

Gateway devices combine an integrated router and a modem in one unit, and connect directly to the ISP service. As with integrated routers, the gateway device receives a public address from the ISP and internal PCs will receive private addresses from the gateway device.

5.4.3 Network Address Translation

Refer to
Figure
in online course

The integrated router receives a public address from the ISP, which allows it to send and receive packets on the Internet. It, in turn, provides private addresses to local network clients. Since private addresses are not allowed on the Internet, a process is needed for translating private addresses into unique public addresses to allow local clients to communicate on the Internet.

The process used to convert private addresses to Internet-routable addresses is called Network Address Translation (*NAT*). With NAT, a private (local) source IP address is translated to a public (global) address. The process is reversed for incoming packets. The integrated router is able to translate many internal IP addresses to the same public address, by using NAT.

Only packets destined for other networks need to be translated. These packets must pass through the gateway, where the integrated router replaces the source host's *private IP address* with its own public IP address.

Although each host on the internal network has a unique private IP address assigned to it, the hosts must share the single Internet routable addressed assigned to the integrated router.

Refer to **Packet Tracer Activity** for this chapter

Packet Tracer Activity

Configure a multi-function device as a DHCP server and configure a client to receive the IP configuration. Verify the configuration of public and private addresses.

Summary

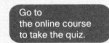

Go to
the online course
to take the quiz.

Quiz

Take the chapter quiz to check your knowledge.

Your Chapter Notes

CHAPTER 6

Network Services

Introduction

Refer to **Figure** in online course

6.1 Clients/Servers and Their Interaction

Refer to **Figure** in online course

6.1.1 Client Server Relationship

Every day, people use the services available over networks and the Internet to communicate with others and to perform routine tasks. We rarely think of the servers, clients and networking devices that are necessary in order for us to receive an email, enter information into a *blog*, or shop for the best bargains in an online store. Most of the commonly used Internet applications rely on complicated interactions between various different servers and clients.

The term server refers to a host running a software application that provides information or services to other hosts connected to the network. A well-known example of an application is a web server. There are millions of servers connected to the Internet, providing services such as web sites, email, financial transactions, music downloads, etc. A factor that is crucial to enabling these complex interactions to function is that they all use agreed standards and protocols.

Refer to **Figure** in online course

To request and view a web page, a person uses a device that is running web client software. A client is the name given to a computer application that someone uses to access information held on a server. A web browser is a good example of a client.

Refer to **Figure** in online course

The key characteristic of client/server systems is that the client sends a request to a server, and the server responds by carrying out a function, such as sending information back to the client. The combination of a web browser and a web server is perhaps the most commonly used instance of a client/server system.

Refer to **Interactive Graphic** in online course.

Activity

Match the service to the client's request.

Drag the appropriate server service to the client to satisfy the client request.

6.1.2 Role of Protocols in Client Server Communication

Refer to **Figure** in online course

A web server and a web client use specific protocols and standards in the process of exchanging information to ensure that the messages are received and understood. These protocols cover: application, transport, Internetwork and network access protocols.

Application Protocol

Hypertext Transfer Protocol (*HTTP*) governs the way that a web server and a web client interact. HTTP defines the format of the requests and responses exchanged between the client and server. HTTP relies on other protocols to govern how the messages are transported between client and server.

Transport Protocol

Transmission Control Protocol (*TCP*) is the transport protocol that manages the individual conversations between web servers and web clients. TCP formats the HTTP messages into segments to be sent to the destination host. It also provides flow control and acknowledgement of packets exchanged between hosts.

Internetwork Protocol

The most common internetwork protocol is Internet Protocol (IP). IP is responsible for taking the formatted segments from TCP, assigning the logical addressing, and encapsulating them into packets for routing to the destination host.

Network Access Protocols

Refer to
Figure
in online course

Ethernet is the most commonly used protocol for local networks. Network access protocols perform two primary functions, data link management and physical network transmissions.

Data link management protocols take the packets from IP and encapsulate them into the appropriate frame format for the local network. These protocols assign the physical addresses to the frames and prepare them to be transmitted over the network.

The standards and protocols for the physical media govern how the bits are represented on the media, how the signals are sent over the media, and how they are interpreted by the receiving hosts. Network interface cards implement the appropriate protocols for the media that is being used.

6.1.3 TCP and UDP Transport Protocols

Refer to
Figure
in online course

Each service available over the network has its own application protocols that are implemented in the server and client software. In addition to the application protocols, all of the common Internet services use Internet Protocol (IP), to address and route messages between source and destination hosts.

IP is concerned only with the structure, addressing and routing of packets. IP does specify how the delivery or transportation of the packets takes place. Transport protocols specify how to transfer messages between hosts. The two most common transport protocols are Transmission Control Protocol (TCP) and User Datagram Protocol (UDP). The IP protocol uses these transport protocols to enable hosts to communicate and transfer data.

Refer to
Figure
in online course

When an application requires acknowledgment that a message is delivered, it uses TCP. This is similar to sending a registered letter through the postal system, where the recipient must sign for the letter to acknowledge its receipt.

TCP breaks up a message into small pieces known as segments. The segments are numbered in sequence and passed to IP process for assembly into packets. TCP keeps track of the number of segments that have been sent to a specific host from a specific application. If the sender does not receive an acknowledgement within a certain period of time, it assumes that the segments were lost and retransmits them. Only the portion of the message that is lost is resent, not the entire message.

On the receiving host, TCP is responsible for reassembling the message segments and passing them to the application.

FTP and HTTP are examples of applications that use TCP to ensure delivery of data.

Refer to
Figure
in online course

In some cases, the TCP acknowledgment protocol is not required and actually slows down information transfer. In those cases, UDP may be a more appropriate transport protocol.

UDP is a 'best effort' delivery system that does not require acknowledgment of receipt. This is similar to sending a standard letter through the postal system. It is not guaranteed that the letter is received, but the chances are good.

UDP is preferable with applications such as streaming audio, video and voice over IP (*VoIP*). Acknowledgments would slow down delivery and retransmissions are undesirable.

An example of an application that uses UDP is Internet radio. If some of the message is lost during its journey over the network, it is not retransmitted. If a few packets are missed, the listener might hear a slight break in the sound. If TCP were used and the lost packets were resent, the transmission would pause to receive them and the disruption would be more noticeable.

Refer to **Interactive Graphic** in online course.

Activity

Match the correct transport protocol to the characteristic described.

Drag the description to the correct transport protocol.

6.1.4 TCP/IP Port Numbers

Refer to **Figure** in online course

When a message is delivered using either TCP or UDP, the protocols and services requested are identified by a port number. A port is a numeric identifier within each *segment* that is used to keep track of specific conversations and destination services requested. Every message that a host sends contains both a source and destination port.

Destination Port

The client places a destination port number in the segment to tell the destination server what service is being requested. For example, Port 80 refers to HTTP or web service. When a client specifies Port 80 in the destination port, the server that receives the message knows that web services are being requested. A server can offer more than one service simultaneously. For example, a server can offer web services on Port 80 at the same time that it offers FTP connection establishment on Port 21.

Source Port

The source port number is randomly generated by the sending device to identify a conversation between two devices. This allows multiple conversations to occur simultaneously. In other words, multiple devices can request HTTP service from a web server at the same time. The separate conversations are tracked based on the source ports.

The source and destination ports are placed within the segment. The segments are then encapsulated within an IP packet. The IP packet contains the IP address of the source and destination. The combination of the source and destination IP address and the source and destination port number is known as a socket. The socket is used to identify the server and service being requested by the client. Every day thousands of hosts communicate with thousands of different servers. Those communications are identified by the sockets.

6.2 Application Protocols and Services

6.2.1 Domain Name Service (DNS)

Refer to **Figure** in online course

Thousands of servers, installed in many different locations, provide the services we use daily over the Internet. Each of these servers is assigned a unique IP address that identifies it on the local network where it is connected.

It would be impossible to remember all of the IP addresses for all of the servers hosting services on the Internet. Instead, there is an easier way to locate servers by associating a name with an IP address.

The Domain Name System (*DNS*) provides a way for hosts to use this name to request the IP address of a specific server. DNS names are registered and organized on the Internet within specific high level groups, or domains. Some of the most common high level domains on the Internet are .com, .edu, and .net.

Refer to
Figure
in online course

A DNS server contains a table that associates hostnames in a domain with corresponding IP addresses. When a client has the name of server, such as a web server, but needs to find the IP address, it sends a request to the DNS server on port 53. The client uses the IP address of the DNS server configured in the DNS settings of the host's IP configuration.

When the DNS server receives the request, it checks its table to determine the IP address associated with that web server. If the local DNS server does not have an entry for the requested name, it queries another DNS server within the domain. When the DNS server learns the IP address, that information is sent back to the client. If the DNS server cannot determine the IP address, the request will time out and the client will not be able to communicate with the web server.

Client software works with the DNS protocol to obtain IP addresses in a way that is transparent to the user.

Refer to
Lab Activity
for this chapter

Lab Activity

Use the `ping` command, a browser and `nslookup` to observe the relationship between domain names and IP addresses.

6.2.2 Web Clients and Servers

Refer to
Figure
in online course

When a web client receives the IP address of a web server, the client browser uses that IP address and port 80 to request web services. This request is sent to the server using the Hypertext Transfer Protocol (HTTP).

When the server receives a port 80 request, the server responds to the client request and sends the web page to the client. The information content of a web page is encoded using specialized 'mark-up' languages. *HTML* (Hypertext Mark-up Language) is the most commonly used but others, such as XML and XHTML, are gaining popularity.

The HTTP protocol is not a secure protocol; information could easily be intercepted by other users as it is sent over the network. In order to provide security for the data, HTTP can be used with secure transport protocols. Requests for secure HTTP are sent to port 443. These requests require the use of https: in the site address in the browser, rather than http:.

There are many different web servers and web clients available on the market. The HTTP protocol and HTML make it possible for these servers and clients from many different manufactures to work together seamlessly.

Refer to **Packet Tracer Activity**
for this chapter

Packet Tracer Activity

Observe traffic requests when a client browser requests web pages from a server.

6.2.3 FTP Clients and Servers

Refer to
Figure
in online course

In addition to web services, another common service used across the Internet is one that allows users to transfer files.

The File Transfer Protocol (FTP) provides an easy method to transfer files from one computer to another. A host running FTP client software can access an FTP server to perform various file management functions including file uploads and downloads.

The FTP server enables a client to exchange files between devices. It also enables clients to manage files remotely by sending file management commands such as delete or rename. To accomplish this, the FTP service uses two different ports to communicate between client and server.

Requests to begin an FTP session are sent to the server using destination port 21. Once the session is opened, the server will change to port 20 to transfer the data files.

FTP client software is built into computer operating systems and into most web browsers. Standalone FTP clients offer many options in an easy-to-use GUI-based interface.

Refer to
Figure
in online course

Lab Activity

Refer to
Lab Activity
for this chapter

Use a FTP client to transfer files from a FTP server.

6.2.4 Email Clients and Servers

Refer to
Figure
in online course

Email is one of the most popular client/server applications on the Internet. Email servers run server software that enables them to interact with clients and with other email servers over the network.

Each mail server receives and stores mail for users who have mailboxes configured on the mail server. Each user with a mailbox must then use an email client to access the mail server and read these messages.

Mail servers are also used to send mail addressed to local mailboxes or mailboxes located on other email servers.

Mailboxes are identified by the format:

user@company.domain.

Various application protocols used in processing email include *SMTP*, *POP3*, IMAP4.

Simple Mail Transfer Protocol (SMTP)

Refer to
Figure
in online course

SMTP is used by an email client to send messages to its local email server. The local server then decides if the message is destined for a local mailbox or if the message is addressed to a mailbox on another server.

If the server has to send the message to a different server, SMTP is used between the two servers as well. SMTP requests are sent to port 25.

Post Office Protocol (POP3)

A server that supports POP clients receives and stores messages addressed to its users. When the client connects to the email server, the messages are downloaded to the client. By default, messages are not kept on the server after they have been accessed by the client. Clients contact POP3 servers on port 110.

Internet Message Access Protocol (IMAP4)

A server that supports IMAP clients also receives and stores messages addressed to its users. However, it keeps the messages in the mailboxes on the server, unless they are deleted by the user. The most current version of IMAP is IMAP4 which listens for client requests on port 143.

Many different email servers exist for the various network operating system platforms.

Refer to
Figure
in online course

An email client connects to the email server to download and view messages. Most email clients can be configured to use either POP3 or IMAP4 depending on the email server where the mailbox is located. Email clients must also be able to send email to the server using SMTP.

Different email servers can be configured for incoming and outgoing mail.

The following are typical entries when configuring an email client:

- POP3 or IMAP4 Server name
- SMTP Server name
- Username
- User password
- SPAM and Virus filters

The graphic shows the basic setup of a POP3 and SMTP email account using *Microsoft Outlook*.

Refer to
Lab Activity
for this chapter

Lab Activity

Configure an email client to access an email server and send and receive email.

6.2.5 IM Clients and Servers

Refer to
Figure
in online course

Instant Messaging (IM) is one of the most popular communication tools in use today. IM software is run locally on each computer and allows users to communicate or chat over the Internet in real-time. Many different IM applications are available from various companies. Each instant messaging service can use a different protocol and destination port, so two hosts must have compatible IM software installed for them to communicate.

IM applications require minimal configuration to operate. Once the client is downloaded all that is required is to enter username and password information. This allows the IM client to authenticate to the IM network. Once logged into the server, clients can send messages to other clients in real-time. In addition to text messages, IM supports the transfer of video, music and speech files. IM clients may have a telephony feature, which allows users to make phone calls over the Internet. Additional configuration can be done to customize the IM client with "Buddy Lists" and a personal look and feel.

IM client software can be downloaded and used on all types of hosts, including: computers, PDAs and cell phones.

6.2.6 Voice Clients and Servers

Refer to
Figure
in online course

Making telephone calls over the Internet is becoming increasingly popular. An Internet telephony client uses peer-to-peer technology similar to that used by instant messaging. IP telephony makes use of Voice over IP (VoIP) technology which uses IP packets to carry digitized voice as data.

To start using Internet telephone, download the client software from one of the companies that provides the service. Rates for Internet telephone services can vary greatly between regions and providers.

When the software has been installed, the user selects a unique name. This is so that calls can be received from other users. Speakers and a microphone, built-in or separate, are required. A headset is frequently plugged into the computer to serve as a phone.

Calls are made to other users of the same service on the Internet, by selecting the username from a list. A call to a regular telephone (land line or cell phone) requires the use of a gateway to access the Public Switched Telephone Network (*PSTN*).

The protocols and destination ports used by Internet telephony applications can vary based on the software.

6.2.7 Port Numbers

Refer to
Figure
in online course

DNS, Web, Email, FTP, IM and VoIP are just some of the many services provided by client/server systems over the Internet. These services may be provided by a single server or by several servers.

In either case, it is necessary for a server to know which service is being requested by a client. Client requests can be identified because the request is made to a specific destination port. Clients are pre-configured to use a destination port that is registered on the Internet for each service.

Ports are broken into three categories and range in number from 1 to 65,535. Ports are assigned and managed by an organization known as the Internet Corporation for Assigned Names and Numbers (ICANN).

Well-Known Ports

Destination ports that are associated with common network applications are identified as well-known ports. These ports are in the range of 1 to 1023.

Registered Ports

Ports 1024 through 49151 can be used as either source or destination ports. These can be used by organizations to register specific applications such as IM applications.

Private Ports

Ports 49152 through 65535, often used as source ports. These ports can be used by any application.

The table shows some of the more common well-known ports.

Refer to
Interactive Graphic
in online course.

Activity

Match the protocol name to the destination port number in the TCP segment.

Click the protocol button based on the destination port number in the TCP segment.

6.3 Layered Model and Protocols

6.3.1 Protocol Interaction

Refer to
Figure
in online course

Successful communication between hosts requires interaction between a numbers of protocols. These protocols are implemented in software and hardware that is loaded on each host and network device.

The interaction between protocols can be depicted as a protocol stack. It shows the protocols as a layered hierarchy, with each higher-level protocol depending on the services of the protocols shown in the lower levels.

The graphic shows a protocol stack with the primary protocols necessary to run a web server over Ethernet. The lower layers of the stack are concerned with moving data over the network and providing services to the upper layers. The upper layers are focused more on the content of the message being sent and the user interface.

Refer to
Figure
in online course

To visualize the interaction between various protocols, it is common use a layered model. A layered model depicts the operation of the protocols occurring within each layer, as well as the interaction with the layers above and below it.

The layered model has many benefits:

- Assists in protocol design, because protocols that operate at a specific layer have defined information that they act upon and a defined interface to the layers above and below.

- Fosters competition because products from different vendors can work together.

- Prevents technology or capability changes in one layer from affecting other layers above and below.

- Provides a common language to describe networking functions and capabilities.

The first layered reference model for internetwork communications was created in the early 1970s and is referred to as the Internet model. It defines four categories of functions that must occur for communications to be successful. The architecture of the TCP/IP protocols follows the structure of this model. Because of this, the Internet model is commonly referred to as the *TCP/IP model*.

6.3.2 Protocol Operation of Sending and Receiving a Message

Refer to
Figure
in online course

When sending messages on a network, the protocol stack on a host operates from top to bottom. In the web server example, a browser on the client requests a web page from a web server on destination port 80. This starts the process of sending the web page to the client.

As the web page is sent down the web server protocol stack, the application data is broken into TCP segments. Each TCP segment is given a header containing a source and destination port.

The TCP segment encapsulates HTTP protocol and web page HTML user data and sends it down to the next protocol layer, which is IP. Here the TCP segment is encapsulated within an IP packet, which adds an IP header. The IP header contains source and destination IP addresses.

Next, the IP packet is sent to the Ethernet protocol where it is encapsulated in a frame header and *trailer*. Each Ethernet frame header contains a source and destination MAC address. The trailer contains error checking information. Finally the bits are encoded onto the Ethernet media (copper or fiber optic cable) by the server NIC.

Refer to
Figure
in online course

When messages are received from the network, the protocol stack on a host operates from bottom to top. Previously, we saw the process of encapsulation at each layer when the web server sent the web page to the client. The process of receiving the web page starts the de-encapsulation of the message by the client.

As the bits are received by the Client NIC, they are decoded and the destination MAC address is recognized by the client as its own.

The frame is sent up the web client protocol stack where the Ethernet header (source and destination MAC addresses) and trailer are removed (de-encapsulated). The remaining IP packet and contents are passed up to the IP layer.

At the IP layer the IP header (source and destination IP addresses) is removed and the contents passed up to the TCP layer.

At the TCP layer the TCP header (source and destination ports) is removed and the web page user data contents are passed up to the Browser application using HTTP. As TCP segments are received they are reassembled to create the web page.

Refer to
Interactive Graphic
in online course.

Activity

Match the host, protocol and encapsulation terminology with the proper protocol or layer.

Drag the term on the right to the appropriate proper protocol or layer.

6.3.3 Open Systems Interconnect Model

Refer to
Figure
in online course

The Open Systems Interconnect Model was developed by the International Organization for Standardization (ISO) in 1984. Unlike the TCP/IP model, it does not specify the interaction of any specific protocols. It was created as architecture for developers to follow to design protocols for network communications. Although very few protocol stacks exactly implement the seven layers of the OSI model, it is now considered the primary reference model for inter-computer communications.

The OSI model includes all functions, or tasks, associated with Inter-network communications, not just those related to the TCP/IP protocols. Compared to the TCP/IP model, which only has four layers, the OSI model organizes the tasks into seven more specific groups. A task, or group of tasks, is then assigned to each of the seven OSI layers.

The essence of protocol stacks is the separation and organization of essential functions. The separation of functions enables each layer in the stack to operate independently of others. For example, it is feasible for a web site to be accessed from a laptop computer connected to a cable modem at home, or from a laptop using wireless, or a web-enabled mobile phone. The Application layer operates seamlessly, regardless of the way the lower layers are operating.

In the same way, the lower layers operate seamlessly. For example, an Internet connection functions satisfactorily when a variety of applications are running at the same time, such as email, web browsing, IM, and music download.

Refer to
Figure
in online course

The Packet Tracer (PT) program graphical interface allows viewing of simulated data being transmitted between two hosts. It uses Protocol Data Units (PDUs) to represent network traffic frames and displays protocol stack information at the appropriate layers of the OSI model.

In the graphic, the request from the Web client is being received by the Ethernet NIC in the Web Server. The following information is shown in OSI layers 1 through 4.

Layer 1 (Physical): Fast Ethernet port

Layer 2 (Data Link): Ethernet Mac addresses

Layer 3 (Network): IP addresses

Layer 4 (Transport): TCP port numbers

Refer to
Interactive Graphic
in online course.

Activity

Match the header address, protocol or term to the proper layer in the network model.

Drag the header address, protocol or term to the appropriate network model layer.

Refer to
Interactive Graphic
in online course.

Activity

Build an Ethernet frame with proper components and send it to its destination.

Drag the source and destination address information to the correct locations in the frame.

Refer to **Packet
Tracer Activity**
for this chapter

Packet Tracer Activity

Use Packet Tracer to view PDU information being sent between a client and server.

Summary

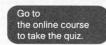

Quiz

Take the chapter quiz to check your knowledge.

Your Chapter Notes

CHAPTER 7

Wireless Technologies

Introduction

Refer to
Figure
in online course

7.1 Wireless Technology

7.1.1 Wireless Technologies and Devices

Refer to
Figure
in online course

In addition to the wired network, various technologies exist that allow the transmission of information between hosts without cables. These are known as wireless technologies.

Wireless technologies use electromagnetic waves to carry information between devices. An electromagnetic wave is the same medium that carries radio signals through the air.

The electromagnetic spectrum includes such things as radio and television broadcast bands, visible light, x-rays and gamma-rays. Each of these has a specific range of wavelengths and associated energies as shown in the diagram.

Some types of electromagnetic waves are not suitable for carrying data. Other parts of the spectrum are regulated by governments and licensed to various organizations for specific applications. Certain areas of the spectrum have been set aside to allow public use without the restriction of having to apply for special permits. The most common wavelengths used for public wireless communications include the Infrared and part of the Radio Frequency (*RF*) band.

Refer to
Figure
in online course

Infrared

Infrared (IR) is relatively low energy and cannot penetrate through walls or other obstacles. However, it is commonly used to connect and move data between devices such as Personal Digital Assistants (PDAs) and PCs. A specialized communication port known as an Infrared Direct Access (*IrDA*) port uses IR to exchange information between devices. IR only allows a one-to-one type of connection.

IR is also used for remote control devices, wireless mice, and wireless keyboards. It is generally used for short-range, line-of-sight, communications. However, it is possible to reflect the IR signal off objects to extend the range. For greater ranges, higher frequencies of electromagnetic waves are required.

Refer to
Figure
in online course

Radio Frequency (RF)

RF waves can penetrate through walls and other obstacles, allowing a much greater range than IR.

Certain areas of the RF bands have been set aside for use by unlicensed devices such as wireless LANs, cordless phones and computer peripherals. This includes the 900 MHz, 2.4 GHz, and the 5

GHz frequency ranges. These ranges are known as the Industrial Scientific and Medical (*ISM*) bands and can be used with very few restrictions.

Bluetooth is a technology that makes use of the 2.4 GHz band. It is limited to low-speed, short-range communications, but has the advantage of communicating with many devices at the same time. This one-to-many communications has made Bluetooth technology the preferred method over IR for connecting computer peripherals such as mice, keyboards and printers.

Other technologies that make use of the 2.4 GHz and 5 GHz bands are the modern wireless LAN technologies that conform to the various IEEE 802.11 standards. They are unlike Bluetooth technology in that they transmit at a much higher power level, which gives them a greater range.

Activity

Refer to Interactive Graphic in online course.

Determine if the type of wireless technology being used is Bluetooth, IR or 802.3 wireless standard.

Drag and drop the appropriate

7.1.2 Benefits and Limitations of Wireless Technology

Refer to Figure in online course

Wireless technology offers many advantages compared to traditional wired networks.

One of the main advantages is the ability to provide anytime, anywhere connectivity. The widespread implementation of wireless in public locations, known as hotspots, allows people to easily connect to the Internet to download information and exchange emails and files.

Wireless technology is fairly easy and inexpensive to install. The cost of home and business wireless devices continues to decrease. Yet, despite the decrease in cost, the data rate and capabilities of these devices have increased, allowing faster, more reliable wireless connections.

Wireless technology enables networks to be easily expanded, without the limitations of cabled connections. New and visiting users can join the network quickly and easily.

Refer to Figure in online course

Despite the flexibility and benefits of wireless, there are some limitations and risks.

First, Wireless LAN (*WLAN*) technologies make use of the unlicensed regions of the RF spectrum. Since these regions are unregulated, many different devices make use of them. As a result, these regions are congested and signals from different devices often interfere with each other. In addition, many devices such as microwave ovens and cordless phones use these frequencies and can interfere with WLAN communications.

Second, a major concern with wireless is security. Wireless provides ease of access. It does this by broadcasting data in a manner that allows anyone the ability to access it. However, this same feature also limits the amount of protection wireless can provide for the data. It allows anyone to intercept the communication stream, even unintended recipients. To address these security concerns, techniques have been developed to help secure wireless transmissions including *encryption* and *authentication*.

7.1.3 Types of Wireless Networks and Their Boundaries

Refer to Figure in online course

Wireless networks are grouped into three major categories: Wireless Personal Area networks (WPAN), Wireless Local Area networks (WLAN), and Wireless Wide Area networks (WWAN).

Despite these distinct categories, it is difficult to place boundary limitations on a wireless implementation. This is because, unlike a wired network, wireless networks do not have precisely defined boundaries. The range of wireless transmissions can vary due to many factors. Wireless networks are susceptible to outside sources of interference, both natural and man-made. Fluctuations in temperature and humidity can greatly alter the coverage of wireless networks. Obstacles within the wireless environment can also affect the range.

Refer to
Figure
in online course

WPAN

This is the smallest wireless network used to connect various peripheral devices such as mice, keyboards and PDAs to a computer. All of these devices are dedicated to a single host with usually use IR or Bluetooth technology.

WLAN

WLAN is typically used to extend the boundaries of the local wired network (LAN). WLANs use RF technology and conform to the IEEE 802.11 standards. They allow many users to connect to a wired network through a device known as an Access Point (AP). An Access Point provides a connection between wireless hosts and hosts on an Ethernet wired network.

WWAN

WWAN networks provide coverage over extremely large areas. A good example of a WWAN is the cell phone network. These networks use technologies such as Code Division Multiple Access (CDMA) or Global System for Mobile Communication (GSM) and are often regulated by government agencies.

Refer to
Interactive Graphic
in online course.

Activity

Classify each scenario as either a WPAN, WLAN or WWAN.

Select the type of network implementation for each scenario.

7.2 Wireless LANs

7.2.1 Wireless LAN Standards

Refer to
Figure
in online course

A number of standards have been developed to ensure that wireless devices can communicate. They specify the RF spectrum used, data rates, how the information is transmitted, and more. The main organization responsible for the creation of wireless technical standards is the IEEE.

The IEEE 802.11 standard governs the WLAN environment. There are four amendments to the IEEE 802.11 standard that describe different characteristics for wireless communications. The currently available amendments are *802.11a*, *802.11b*, *802.11g* and *802.11n* (802.11n is not ratified at the time of this writing). Collectively these technologies are referred to as Wi-Fi, Wireless Fidelity.

Another organization, known as the Wi-Fi Alliance, is responsible for testing wireless LAN devices from different manufacturers. The Wi-Fi logo on a device means that this equipment meets standards and should interoperate with other devices of the same standard.

Refer to
Figure
in online course

802.11a:

- Uses 5 GHz RF spectrum

- Not compatible with 2.4 GHz spectrum, i.e. 802.11 b/g/n devices

- Range is approximately 33% that of the 802.11 b/g

- Relatively expensive to implement compared to other technologies

- Increasingly difficult to find 802.11a compliant equipment

802.11b:

- First of the 2.4 GHz technologies

- Maximum data-rate of 11 Mbps

- Range of approximately 46 m (150 ft) indoors/96 m (300 ft) outdoors

802.11g:

- 2.4 GHz technologies

- Maximum data-rate increase to 54 Mbps

- Same range as the 802.11b

- Backwards compatible with 802.11b

802.11n:

- Newest standard in development

- 2.4 GHz technologies (draft standard specifies support for 5 GHz)

- Extends the range and data *throughput*

- Backwards compatible with existing 802.11g and 802.11b equipment (draft standard specifies 802.11a support)

7.2.2 Wireless LAN Components

Refer to
Figure
in online course

Once a standard is adopted, it is important that all components within the WLAN adhere to the standard, or are at least compatible with the standard. There are various components that must be considered in a WLAN including: a *wireless client* or *STA*, an Access Point, a Wireless Bridge and an antenna.

Refer to
Figure
in online course

Antennas:

- Used on APs and Wireless bridges

- Increases the output signal strength from a wireless device

- Receives wireless signals from other devices such as STAs

- Increase in signal strength from an antenna is known as the gain

- Higher gains usually translate into increased transmission distances

Antennas are classified according to the way they radiate the signal. Directional antennas concentrate the signal strength into one direction. Omni-directional antennas are designed to emit equally in all directions.

By concentrating all of the signal into one direction, directional antennas can achieve great transmission distances. Directional antennas are normally used in bridging applications while omni-directional antennas are found on APs.

Refer to
Interactive Graphic
in online course.

Activity

Match the WLAN component to its functionality.

Drag the descriptive terms to the proper device.

7.2.3 WLANs and the SSID

Refer to
Figure
in online course

When building a wireless network, it is important that the wireless components connect to the appropriate WLAN. This is done using a Service Set Identifier (*SSID*).

The SSID is a case-sensitive, alpha-numeric string that is up to 32-characters. It is sent in the header of all frames transmitted over the WLAN. The SSID is used to tell wireless devices which WLAN they belong to and with which other devices they can communicate.

Regardless of the type of WLAN installation, all wireless devices in a WLAN must be configured with the same SSID in order to communicate.

Refer to
Figure
in online course

There are two basic forms of WLAN installations: Ad-hoc and infrastructure mode.

Ad-hoc

The simplest form of a wireless network is created by connecting two or more wireless clients together in a peer-to-peer network. A wireless network established in this manner is known as an ad-hoc network and does not include an AP. All clients within an ad-hoc network are equal. The area covered by this network is known as an Independent Basic Service Set (*IBSS*). A simple ad-hoc network can be used to exchange files and information between devices without the expense and complexity of purchasing and configuring an AP.

Infrastructure Mode

Although an ad-hoc arrangement may be good for small networks, larger networks require a single device that controls communications in the wireless cell. If present, an AP will take over this role and control who can talk and when. This is known as infrastructure mode and is the mode of wireless communication most often used in the home and business environment. In this form of WLAN, individual STAs can not communicate directly with each other. To communicate, each device must obtain permission from the AP. The AP controls all communications and ensures that all STAs have equal access to the medium. The area covered by a single AP is known as a Basic Service Set (BSS) or cell.

Refer to
Figure
in online course

The Basic Service Set (*BSS*) is the smallest building block of a WLAN. The area of coverage of a single AP is limited. To expand the coverage area, it is possible to connect multiple BSSs through a Distribution System (DS). This forms an Extended Service Set (*ESS*). An ESS uses multiple APs. Each AP is in a separate BSS.

In order to allow movement between the cells without the loss of signal, BSSs must overlap by approximately 10%. This allows the client to connect to the second AP before disconnecting from the first AP.

Most home and small business environments consist of a single BSS. However, as the required coverage area and number hosts needing to connect increases it becomes necessary to create an ESS.

Refer to
Interactive Graphic
in online course.

Activity

Set the SSID on an AP using the GUI interface.

7.2.4 Wireless Channels

Refer to
Figure
in online course

Regardless if the wireless clients are communicating within an IBSS, BSS or ESS the conversation between sender and receiver must be controlled. One way this is accomplished is through the use of Channels.

Channels are created by dividing up the available RF spectrum. Each channel is capable of carrying a different conversation. This is similar to the way that multiple television channels are transmitted across a single medium. Multiple APs can function in close proximity to one another as long as they use different channels for communication.

Unfortunately it is possible for the frequencies used by some channels to overlap with those used by others. Different conversations must be carried on non-overlapping channels. The number and distribution of channels vary by region and technology. The selection of channel used for a specific conversation can be set manually or automatically, based on factors such as current usage and available throughput.

Normally each wireless conversation makes use of a separate channel. Some of the newer technologies combine the channels to create a single wide channel, which provides more bandwidth and increases the data rate.

Refer to
Figure
in online course

Within a WLAN, the lack of well-defined boundaries makes it impossible to detect if collisions occur during transmission. Therefore, it is necessary to use an access method on a wireless network that ensures collisions do not occur.

Wireless technology uses an access method called Carrier Sense Multiple Access with Collision Avoidance (***CSMA/CA***). CSMA/CA creates a reservation on the channel for use by a specific conversation. While a reservation is in place, no other device may transmit on the channel thus possible collisions are avoided.

How does this reservation process work? If a device requires use of a specific communication channel in a BSS, it must ask permission from the AP. This is known as a Request to Send (***RTS***). If the channel is available, the AP will respond to the device with a Clear to Send (***CTS***) message indicating that the device may transmit on the channel. A CTS is broadcast to all devices within the BSS. Therefore, all devices in the BSS know that the requested channel is now in use.

Once the conversation is complete, the device that requested the channel sends another message to the AP known as an Acknowledgement (***ACK***). The ACK indicates to the AP that the channel can be released. This message is also broadcast to all devices on the WLAN. All devices within the BSS receive the ACK and know that the channel is once again available.

Refer to
Interactive Graphic
in online course.

Activity

Configure the channels used by an AP using the GUI interface.

7.2.5 Configuring the Access Point

Refer to
Figure
in online course

Once the choice of wireless standard, layout and channel assignment have been made it is time to configure the AP.

Most integrated routers offer both wired and wireless connectivity and serve as the AP in the wireless network. Basic configuration settings such as passwords, IP addresses, and DHCP settings are the same whether the device is being used to connect wired or wireless hosts. Basic configuration tasks, such as changing the default password, should be conducted before the AP is connected to a live network.

When using the wireless functionality of an integrated router, additional configuration parameters are required, such as setting the wireless mode, SSID, and wireless channels to be used.

Refer to
Figure
in online course

Wireless Mode

Most home AP devices can support various modes, mainly 802.11b, 802.11g and 802.11n. Although these all use the 2.4 GHz range, each uses a different technology to obtain its maximum throughput. The type of mode enabled on the AP depends on the type of host connecting to it. If only one type of host connects to the AP device, set the mode to support it. If multiple types of hosts will connect, select mixed mode. Each mode includes a certain amount of overhead. By enabling mixed mode, network performance will decrease due to the overhead incurred in supporting all modes.

SSID

The SSID is used to identify the WLAN. All devices that wish to participate in the WLAN must use the same SSID. To allow easy detection of the WLAN by clients, the SSID is broadcast. It is possible to disable the broadcast feature of the SSID. If the SSID is not broadcast; wireless clients will need to have this value manually configured.

Wireless Channel

The choice of channel for an AP must be made relative to the other wireless networks around it. Adjacent BSSs must use non-overlapping channels in order to optimize throughput. Most APs now offer a choice to manually configure the channel or allow the AP to automatically locate the least congested channel or locate the one that offers maximum throughput.

Refer to
Lab Activity
for this chapter

Lab Activity

Configure basic wireless functionality on an AP using the GUI interface.

7.2.6 Configuring the Wireless Client

Refer to
Figure
in online course

A wireless host, or STA, is defined as any device that contains a wireless NIC and wireless client software. This client software allows the hardware to participate in the WLAN. Devices that are STAs include: PDAs, laptops, desktop PCs, printers, projectors and Wi-Fi phones.

In order for a STA to connect to the WLAN, the client configuration must match that of the AP. This includes the SSID, security settings, and channel information if the channel was manually set on the AP. These settings are specified in the client software that manages the client connection.

The wireless client software used can be software integrated into the device operating system, or can be a stand-alone, downloadable, wireless utility software specifically designed to interact with the wireless NIC.

Refer to
Figure
in online course

Integrated Wireless Utility Software

The Windows XP wireless client software is an example of a popular wireless client utility that is included as part of the device OS. This client software is basic management software that can control most wireless client configurations. It is user friendly and offers a simple connection process.

Stand-alone Wireless Utility Software

Wireless utility software, such as that supplied with the wireless NIC, is designed to work with that specific NIC. It usually offers enhanced functionality over Windows XP wireless utility software including feature such as:

- **Link Information** - displays the current strength and quality of a wireless single

- **Profiles** - allows configuration options such as channel and SSID to be specified for each wireless network

- **Site Survey** - enables the detection of all wireless networks in the vicinity

It is not possible to allow both the wireless utility software and Windows XP client software to manage the wireless connection at the same time. For most situations Windows XP is sufficient. However, if multiple profiles must be created for each wireless network or advanced configurations settings are necessary, it is better to use the utility supplied with the NIC.

Refer to
Figure
in online course

Once the client software is configured, verify the link between the client and the AP.

Open the wireless link information screen to display information such as the connection data rate, connection status, and wireless channel used. The Link Information feature, if available, displays the current signal strength and quality of the wireless signal.

In addition to verifying the wireless connection status, verify that data can actually be transmitted. One of the most common tests for verifying successful data transmission is the Ping test. If the ping is successful, data transmission is possible.

If the ping is unsuccessful from source to destination, then ping the AP from the wireless client to ensure that wireless connectivity is available. If this fails as well, the issue is between the wireless client and the AP. Check the setting information and try to reestablish connectivity.

If the wireless client can successfully connect to the AP, then check the connectivity from the AP to the next hop on the path to the destination. If this is successful, then the problem is most likely not with the AP configuration, but may be an issue with another device on the path to the destination or the destination device itself.

Refer to
Lab Activity
for this chapter

Lab Activity

Configure a wireless client to connect to the previously configured AP and verify connectivity.

7.3 Security Considerations on A Wireless LAN

7.3.1 Why People Attack WLANs

Refer to
Figure
in online course

One of the primary benefits of wireless networking is ease and convenience of connecting devices. Unfortunately that ease of connectivity and the fact that the information is transmitted through the air also makes your network vulnerable to interception and attacks.

With wireless connectivity, the attacker does not need a physical connection to your computer or any of your devices to access your network. It is possible for an attacker to tune into signals from your wireless network, much like tuning into a radio station.

The attacker can access your network from any location your wireless signal reaches. Once they have access to your network, they can use your Internet services for free, as well as access computers on the network to damage files, or steal personal and private information.

These vulnerabilities in wireless networking require special security features and implementation methods to help protect your WLAN from attacks. These include simple steps performed during initial setup of the wireless device, as well as more advanced security configurations.

Refer to
Figure
in online course

One easy way to gain entry to a wireless network is through the network name, or SSID.

All computers connecting to the wireless network must know the SSID. By default, wireless routers and access points broadcast SSIDs to all computers within the wireless range. With SSID broadcast activated, any wireless client can detect the network and connect to it, if no other security features are in place.

The SSID broadcast feature can be turned off. When it is turned off, the fact that the network is there is no longer made public. Any computer trying to connect to the network must already know the SSID.

Refer to
Figure
in online course

Additionally, it is important to change the default setting. Wireless devices are shipped preconfigured with settings such as SSIDs, passwords, and IP addresses in place. These defaults make it easy for an attacker to identify and infiltrate a network.

Even with SSID broadcasting disabled, it is possible for someone to get into your network using the well-known default SSID. Additionally, if other default settings, such as passwords and IP addresses are not changed, attackers can access an AP and make changes themselves. Default information should be changed to something more secure and unique.

These changes, by themselves, will not protect your network. For example, SSIDs are transmitted in clear text. There are devices that will intercept wireless signals and read clear text messages. Even with SSID broadcast turned off and default values changed, attackers can learn the name of a wireless network through the use of these devices that intercept wireless signals. This information will be used to connect to the network. It takes a combination of several methods to protect your WLAN.

7.3.2 Limiting Access to a WLAN

Refer to **Figure** in online course

One way to limit access to your wireless network is to control exactly which devices can gain access to your network. This can be accomplished through filtering of the MAC address.

MAC Address Filtering

MAC address filtering uses the MAC address to identify which devices are allowed to connect to the wireless network. When a wireless client attempts to connect, or associate, with an AP it will send MAC address information. If *MAC filtering* is enabled, the wireless router or AP will look up its MAC address a preconfigured list. Only devices whose MAC addresses have been prerecorded in the router's database will be allowed to connect.

If the MAC address is not located in the database, the device will not be allowed to connect to or communicate across the wireless network.

There are some issues with this type of security. For example, it requires the MAC addresses of all devices that should have access to the network be included in the database before connection attempts occur. A device that is not identified in the database will not be able to connect. Additionally, it is possible for an attacker's device to clone the MAC address of another device that has access.

7.3.3 Authentication on a WLAN

Refer to **Figure** in online course

Another way to control who can connect is to implement authentication. Authentication is the process of permitting entry to a network based on a set of credentials. It is used to verify that the device attempting to connect to the network is trusted.

The use of a username and password is a most common form of authentication. In a wireless environment, authentication still ensures that the connected host is verified, but handles the verification process in a slightly different manner. Authentication, if enabled, must occur before the client is allowed to connect to the WLAN. There are three types of wireless authentication methods: *open authentication*, *PSK* and *EAP*.

Open Authentication

By default, wireless devices do not require authentication. Any and all clients are able to associate regardless of who they are. This is referred to as open authentication. Open authentication should only be used on public wireless networks such as those found in many schools and restaurants. It can also be used on networks where authentication will be done by other means once connected to the network.

Refer to **Figure** in online course

Pre-shared keys (PSK)

With PSK both the AP and client must be configured with the same key or secret word. The AP sends a random string of bytes to the client. The client accepts the string, encrypts it (or scrambles it) based on the key, and sends it back to the AP. The AP gets the encrypted string and uses its key to decrypt (or unscramble) it. If the decrypted string received from the client matches the original string sent to the client, the client is allowed to connect.

PSK performs one-way authentication, that is, the host authenticates to the AP. PSK does not authenticate the AP to the host, nor does it authenticate the actual user of the host.

Extensible Authentication Protocol (EAP)

EAP provides mutual, or two-way, authentication as well as user authentication. When EAP software is installed on the client, the client communicates with a backend authentication server such as Remote Authentication Dial-in User Service (*RADIUS*). This backend server functions separately from the AP and maintains a database of valid users that can access the network. When using EAP, the user, not just the host, must provide a username and password which is checked against the RADIUS database for validity. If valid, the user is authenticated.

Refer to
Figure
in online course

Once authentication is enabled, regardless of the method used, the client must successfully pass authentication before it can associate with the AP. If both authentication and MAC address filtering are enabled, authentication occurs first.

Once authentication is successful, the AP will then check the MAC address against the MAC address table. Once verified, the AP adds the host MAC address into its host table. The client is then said to be associated with the AP and can connect to the network.

7.3.4 Encryption on a WLAN

Refer to
Figure
in online course

Authentication and MAC filtering may stop an attacker from connecting to a wireless network but it will not prevent them from being able to intercept transmitted data. Since there are no distinct boundaries on a wireless network, and all traffic is transmitted through the air, it is easy for an attacker to intercept, or sniff, the wireless frames. Encryption is the process of transforming data so that even if it is intercepted it is unusable.

Wired Equivalency Protocol (*WEP*)

Wired Equivalency Protocol (WEP) is an advanced security feature that encrypts network traffic as it travels through the air. WEP uses pre-configured keys to encrypt and decrypt data.

A WEP key is entered as a string of numbers and letters and is generally 64 bits or 128 bits long. In some cases, WEP supports 256 bit keys as well. To simplify creating and entering these keys, many devices include a Passphrase option. The passphrase is an easy way to remember the word or phrase used to automatically generate a key.

In order for WEP to function, the AP, as well as every wireless device allowed to access the network must have the same WEP key entered. Without this key, devices will not be able to understand the wireless transmissions.

Refer to
Figure
in online course

WEP is a great way to prevent attackers from intercepting data. However, there are weaknesses within WEP, including the use of a static key on all WEP enabled devices. There are applications available to attackers that can be used to discover the WEP key. These applications are readily available on the Internet. Once the attacker has extracted the key, they have complete access to all transmitted information.

One way to overcome this vulnerability is to change the key frequently. Another way is to use a more advanced and secure form of encryption known as Wi-Fi Protected Access (*WPA*).

Wi-Fi Protected Access (WPA)

WPA also uses encryption keys from 64 bits up to 256 bits. However, WPA, unlike WEP, generates new, dynamic keys each time a client establishes a connection with the AP. For this reason, WPA is considered more secure than WEP because it is significantly more difficult to crack.

Refer to
Interactive Graphic
in online course.

Activity

Configure encryption using the Linksys GUI interface.

7.3.5 Traffic Filtering on a WLAN

Refer to
Figure
in online course

In addition to controlling who can gain access to the WLAN and who can make use of transmitted data, it is also worthwhile to control the types of traffic transmitted across a WLAN. This is accomplished using traffic filtering.

Traffic filtering blocks undesirable traffic from entering or leaving the wireless network. Filtering is done by the AP as traffic passes through it. It can be used to remove traffic from, or destined to, a specific MAC or IP address. It can also block certain applications by port numbers. By removing unwanted, undesirable and suspicious traffic from the network, more bandwidth is devoted to the movement of important traffic and improves the performance of the WLAN. For example, traffic filtering can be used to block all telnet traffic destined for a specific machine, such as an authentication server. Any attempts to telnet into the authentication server would be considered suspicious and blocked.

Refer to
Lab Activity
for this chapter

Lab Activity

Configure security on an AP using the GUI interface. Configure the client to connect to the secured AP.

7.4 Configuring an Integrated AP and Wireless Client

7.4.1 Planning the WLAN

Refer to
Figure
in online course

When implementing a wireless network solution, it is important to plan before performing any installation. This includes:

- Determining the type of wireless standard to use
- Determining the most efficient layout of devices
- An installation and security plan
- A strategy for backing up and updating the *firmware* of the wireless devices

Wireless Standard

It is necessary to consider several factors when determining which WLAN standard to use. The most common factors include: bandwidth requirements, coverage areas, existing implementations, and cost. This information is gathered by determining end-user requirements.

The best way to learn end-user requirements is to ask questions.

- What throughput is actually required by the applications running on the network?
- How many users will access the WLAN?

- What is the necessary coverage area?

- What is the existing network structure?

- What is the budget?

Refer to
Figure
in online course

The bandwidth available in a BSS must be shared between all the users in that BSS. Even if the applications do not require a high-speed connection, one of the higher-speed technologies may be necessary if multiple users are connecting at the same time.

Different standards support different coverage areas. The 2.4 GHz signal, used in 802.11 b/g/n technologies, travels a greater distance than does the 5 GHz signal, used in 802.11a technologies. Thus 802.11 b/g/n supports a larger BSS. This translates into less equipment and a lower cost of implementation.

The existing network also affects new implementation of WLAN standards. For example, the 802.11n standard is backward compatible with 802.11g and 802.11b but not with 802.11a. If the existing network infrastructure and equipment support 802.11a, new implementations must also support the same standard.

Cost is also a factor. When considering cost, consider Total Cost of Ownership (TCO) which includes the purchase of the equipment as well as installation and support costs. In a medium to large business environment, TCO has a greater impact on the WLAN standard chosen than in the home or small business environment. This is because in the medium to large business, more equipment is necessary and installation plans are required, increasing cost.

Refer to
Figure
in online course

Installation of Wireless Devices

For home or small business environments, the installation usually consists of a limited amount of equipment which can be easily relocated to provide optimum coverage and throughput.

In the enterprise environment, equipment cannot be easily relocated and coverage must be complete. It is important to determine the optimum number and location of APs to provide this coverage at the least amount of cost.

In order to accomplish this, a *site survey* is usually conducted. The person responsible for the site survey must be knowledgeable in WLAN design and equipped with sophisticated equipment for measuring signal strengths and interference. Depending on the size of the WLAN implementation, this can be a very expensive process. For small installations a simple site survey is usually conducted by simply using wireless STAs and the utility programs packaged with most wireless NICs.

In all cases, it is necessary to consider known sources of interference such as high-voltage wires, motors, and other wireless devices when determining the placement of WLAN equipment.

7.4.2 Installing and Securing the AP

Refer to
Figure
in online course

Once the best technology and placement of the AP is determined, install the WLAN device and configure the AP with security measure. Security measures should be planned and configured before connecting the AP to the network or ISP.

Some of the more basic security measures include:

- Change default values for the SSID, usernames and passwords

- Disable broadcast SSID

- Configure MAC Address Filtering

Some of the more advanced security measures include:

- Configure encryption using WEP or WPA
- Configure authentication
- Configure traffic filtering

Keep in mind that no single security measure will keep your wireless network completely secure. Combining multiple techniques will strengthen the integrity of your security plan.

When configuring the clients, it is essential that the SSID matches the SSID configured on the AP. Additionally, encryption keys and authentication keys must also match.

7.4.3 Backing-up and Restoring Configuration Files

Refer to Figure in online course

Configuration Backups

Once the wireless network is properly configured and traffic is moving, a full configuration backup should be performed on wireless devices. This is especially important if a great deal of customization is done to the configuration.

With most integrated routers designed for the home and small business markets, this is simply a matter of selecting the **Backup Configurations** option from the appropriate menu and specifying the location where the file should be saved. The integrated router provides a default name for the configuration file. This file name can be changed.

The restore process is just as simple. Select the **Restore Configurations** option. Then, simply browse to the location where the configuration file was previously saved and select the file. Once the file is selected, click **Start to Restore** to load the configuration file.

Sometimes it may be necessary to return the setting to the factory default conditions. To accomplish this select either the **Restore Factory Defaults** option from the appropriate menu or press and hold the RESET button located for 30 seconds. The latter technique is especially useful if you are unable to connect to the AP of the integrated router through the network but have physical access to the device.

Refer to Interactive Graphic in online course.

Activity

Backup and restore the configurations using the Linksys GUI.

7.4.4 Updating the Firmware

Refer to Figure in online course

Updating the Firmware

The operating system on most integrated routers is stored in firmware. As new features are developed or problems with the existing firmware are discovered, it may become necessary to update the firmware on the device.

The process for updating firmware on an integrated router, such as the Linksys wireless router, is simple. However, it is important that once the process is started, it is not interrupted. If the update process is interrupted before completion, the device may be rendered non-operable.

Determine the version of the firmware currently installed on the device. This information is usually displayed on the configuration screen or the connection status screen. Next, search the manufacturer's web site and related news groups on the Internet to discover the firmware feature set, issues that may warrant an upgrade, and whether updates are available.

Download the updated version of the firmware and store it on the hard drive of a device that can be directly connected to the integrated router. It is better if the machine is directly connected to the integrated router with a cable to prevent any interruption in the update process caused by a wireless connection.

Select the **Firmware Upgrade** feature in the GUI. Browse to the appropriate file on the directly connected device and start the upgrade.

Refer to
Interactive Graphic
in online course.

Activity

Update the Access Point with a new version of the firmware.

Summary

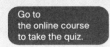
Go to
the online course
to take the quiz.

Quiz

Take the chapter quiz to check your knowledge.

Your Chapter Notes

CHAPTER 8

Basic Security

Introduction

Refer to
Figure
in online course

8.1 Networking threats

Refer to
Figure
in online course

8.1.1 Risks of Network Intrusion

Whether wired or wireless, computer networks are quickly becoming essential to everyday activities. Individuals and organizations alike depend on their computers and networks for functions such as email, accounting, organization and file management. Intrusion by an unauthorized person can result in costly network outages and loss of work. Attacks to a network can be devastating and can result in a loss of time and money due to damage or theft of important information or assets.

Intruders can gain access to a network through software vulnerabilities, hardware attacks or even through less high-tech methods, such as guessing someone's username and password. Intruders who gain access by modifying software or exploiting software vulnerabilities are often called **hackers**.

Once the hacker gains access to the network, four types of threat may arise:

- Information theft
- Identity theft
- Data loss / manipulation
- Disruption of service

Refer to
Lab Activity
for this chapter

Lab Activity

Match the term to the security threat scenario description.

For each security threat scenario displayed, select the answer that most closely matches the scenario.

8.1.2 Sources of Network Intrusion

Security threats from network intruders can come from both internal and external sources.

Refer to
Figure
in online course

External Threats

External threats arise from individuals working outside of an organization. They do not have authorized access to the computer systems or network. External attackers work their way into a network mainly from the Internet, wireless links or dialup access servers.

Internal Threats

Internal threats occur when someone has authorized access to the network through a user account or have physical access to the network equipment. The internal attacker knows the internal politics and people. They often know what information is both valuable and vulnerable and how to get to it.

However, not all internal attacks are intentional. In some cases, an internal threat can come from a trustworthy employee who picks up a virus or security threat, while outside the company and unknowingly brings it into the internal network.

Most companies spend considerable resources defending against external attacks however most threats are from internal sources. According to the FBI, internal access and misuse of computers systems account for approximately 70% of reported incidents of security breaches.

8.1.3 Social Engineering and Phishing

Refer to
Figure
in online course

One of the easiest ways for an intruder to gain access, whether internal or external is by exploiting human behavior. One of the more common methods of exploiting human weaknesses is called Social Engineering.

Social Engineering

Social engineering is a term that refers to the ability of something or someone to influence the behavior of a group of people. In the context of computer and network security Social Engineering refers to a collection of techniques used to deceive internal users into performing specific actions or revealing confidential information.

With these techniques, the attacker takes advantage of unsuspecting legitimate users to gain access to internal resources and private information, such as bank account numbers or passwords.

Social engineering attacks exploit the fact that users are generally considered one of the weakest links in security. Social engineers can be internal or external to the organization, but most often do not come face-to-face with their victims.

Three of the most commonly used techniques in *social engineering* are: *pretexting*, *phishing*, and *vishing*.

Refer to
Figure
in online course

Pretexting

Pretexting is a form of social engineering where an invented scenario (the pretext) is used on a victim in order to get the victim to release information or perform an action. The target is typically contacted over the telephone. For pretexting to be effective, the attacker must be able to establish legitimacy with the intended target, or victim. This often requires some prior knowledge or research on the part of the attacker. For example, if an attacker knows the target's social security number, they may use that information to gain the trust of their target. The target is then more likely to release further information.

Phishing

Phishing is a form of social engineering where the phisher pretends to represent a legitimate outside organization. They typically contact the target individual (the phishee) via email. The phisher might ask for verification of information, such as passwords or usernames in order prevent some terrible consequence from occurring.

Vishing / Phone Phishing

A new form of social engineering that uses Voice over IP (VoIP) is known as vishing. With vishing, an unsuspecting user is sent a voice mail instructing them to call a number which appears to be a legitimate telephone-banking service. The call is then intercepted by a thief. Bank account numbers or passwords entered over the phone for verification are then stolen.

8.2 Methods of attack

8.2.1 Viruses, Worms, and Trojan Horses

Refer to
Figure
in online course

Social engineering is a common security threat which preys upon human weakness to obtain desired results.

In addition to social engineering, there are other types of attacks which exploit the vulnerabilities in computer software. Examples of these attack techniques include: viruses, worms and Trojan horses. All of these are types of malicious software introduced onto a host. They can damage a system, destroy data, as well as deny access to networks, systems, or services. They can also forward data and personal details from unsuspecting PC users to criminals. In many cases, they can replicate themselves and spread to other hosts connected to the network.

Sometimes these techniques are used in combination with social engineering to trick an unsuspecting user into executing the attack.

Refer to
Figure
in online course

Viruses

A virus is a program that runs and spreads by modifying other programs or files. A virus cannot start by itself; it needs to be activated. Once activated, a virus may do nothing more than replicate itself and spread. Though simple, even this type of virus is dangerous as it can quickly use all available memory and bring a system to a halt. A more serious virus may be programmed to delete or corrupt specific files before spreading. Viruses can be transmitted via email attachments, downloaded files, instant messages or via diskette, CD or USB devices.

Worms

A worm is similar to a virus, but unlike a virus does not need to attach itself to an existing program. A worm uses the network to send copies of itself to any connected hosts. Worms can run independently and spread quickly. They do not necessarily require activation or human intervention. Self-spreading network worms can have a much greater impact than a single virus and can infect large parts of the Internet quickly.

Trojan Horses

A *Trojan horse* is a non-self replicating program that is written to appear like a legitimate program, when in fact it is an attack tool. A Trojan horse relies upon its legitimate appearance to deceive the victim into initiating the program. It may be relatively harmless or can contain code that can damage the contents of the computer's hard drive. Trojans can also create a back door into a system allowing hackers to gain access.

Refer to
Lab Activity
for this chapter

Lab Activity

Determine if the user has been infected by a virus, worm or Trojan horse.

Select virus, worm or Trojan horse for each scenario.

8.2.2 Denial of Service and Brute Force Attacks

Refer to
Figure
in online course

Sometimes the goal of an attacker is to shut down the normal operations of a network. This type of attack is usually carried out with the intent to disrupt the functions of an organization.

Denial of Service (*DoS*)

DoS attacks are aggressive attacks on an individual computer or groups of computers with the intent to deny services to intended users. DoS attacks can target end user systems, servers, routers, and network links.

In general, DoS attacks seek to:

- Flood a system or network with traffic to prevent legitimate network traffic from flowing

- Disrupt connections between a client and server to prevent access to a service

There are several types of DoS attacks. Security administrators need to be aware of the types of DoS attacks that can occur and ensure that their networks are protected. Two common DoS attacks are:

- SYN (synchronous) Flooding: a flood of packets are sent to a server requesting a client connection. The packets contain invalid source IP addresses. The server becomes occupied trying to respond to these fake requests and therefore cannot respond to legitimate ones.

- Ping of death: a packet that is greater in size than the maximum allowed by IP (65,535 bytes) is sent to a device. This can cause the receiving system to crash.

> Refer to
> **Figure**
> in online course

Distributed Denial of Service (*DDoS*)

DDoS is a more sophisticated and potentially damaging form of the DoS attack. It is designed to saturate and overwhelm network links with useless data. DDoS operates on a much larger scale than DoS attacks. Typically hundreds or thousands of attack points attempt to overwhelm a target simultaneously. The attack points may be unsuspecting computers that have been previously infected by the DDoS code. The systems that are infected with the DDoS code attack the target site when invoked.

Brute Force

Not all attacks that cause network outages are specifically DoS attacks. A Brute force attack is another type of attack that may result in denial of services.

With brute force attacks, a fast computer is used to try to guess passwords or to decipher an encryption code. The attacker tries a large number of possibilities in rapid succession to gain access or crack the code. Brute force attacks can cause a denial of service due to excessive traffic to a specific resource or by locking out user accounts.

> Refer to
> **Interactive Graphic**
> in online course.

Activity

Attempt to establish a TCP connection to the web server during a Denial of Service (DoS) attack.

Click one of the Inside User client PCs to obtain a TCP connection to the server.

8.2.3 Spyware, Tracking Cookies, Adware and Popups

> Refer to
> **Figure**
> in online course

Not all attacks do damage or prevent legitimate users from having access to resources. Many threats are designed to collect information about users which can be used for advertising, marketing and research purposes. These include Spyware, Tracking Cookies, Adware and Popups. While these may not damage a computer, they invade privacy and can be annoying.

Spyware

Spyware is any program that gathers personal information from your computer without your permission or knowledge. This information is sent to advertisers or others on the Internet and can include passwords and account numbers.

Spyware is usually installed unknowingly when downloading a file, installing another program or clicking a *popup*. It can slow down a computer and make changes to internal settings creating more vulnerabilities for other threats. In addition, *spyware* can be very difficult to remove.

Tracking Cookies

Cookies are a form of spyware but are not always bad. They are used to record information about an Internet user when they visit websites. Cookies may be useful or desirable by allowing personalization and other time saving techniques. Many web sites require that cookies be enabled in order to allow the user to connect.

Refer to
Figure
in online course

Adware

Adware is a form of spyware used to collect information about a user based on websites the user visits. That information is then used for targeted advertising. Adware is commonly installed by a user in exchange for a "free" product. When a user opens a browser window, Adware can start new browser instances which attempt to advertize products or services based on a user's surfing practices. The unwanted browser windows can open repeatedly, and can make surfing the Internet very difficult, especially with slow Internet connections. Adware can be very difficult to uninstall.

Popups and pop-unders

Popups and pop-unders are additional advertising windows that display when visiting a web site. Unlike Adware, popups and pop-unders are not intended to collect information about the user and are typically associated only with the web-site being visited.

- Popups: open in front of the current browser window.

- Pop-unders: open behind the current browser window.

They can be annoying and usually advertise products or services that are undesirable.

8.2.4 Spam

Refer to
Figure
in online course

Another annoying by-product of our increasing reliance on electronic communications is unwanted bulk email. Sometimes merchants do not want to bother with targeted marketing. They want to send their email advertising to as many end users as possible hoping that someone is interested in their product or service. This widely distributed approach to marketing on the Internet is called *spam*.

Spam is a serious network threat that can overload ISPs, email servers and individual end-user systems. A person or organization responsible for sending spam is called a spammer. Spammers often make use of unsecured email servers to forward email. Spammers can use hacking techniques, such as viruses, worms and Trojan horses to take control of home computers. These computers are then used to send spam without the owner's knowledge. Spam can be sent via email or more recently via Instant messaging software.

It is estimated that every user on the Internet receives over 3,000 spam emails in a year. Spam consumes large amounts of Internet bandwidth and is a serious enough problem that many countries now have laws governing spam use.

8.3 Security Policy

8.3.1 Common Security Measures

Refer to
Figure
in online course

Security risks cannot be eliminated or prevented completely. However, effective risk management and assessment can significantly minimize the existing security risks. To minimize the amount of risk, it is important to understand that no single product can make an organization secure. True network security comes from a combination of products and services, combined with a thorough *security policy* and a commitment to adhere to that policy.

A security policy is a formal statement of the rules that users must adhere to when accessing technology and information assets. It can be as simple as an acceptable use policy, or can be several hundred pages in length, and detail every aspect of user connectivity and network usage procedures. A security policy should be the central point for how a network is secured, monitored, tested and improved upon. While most home users do not have a formal written security policy, as a network grows in size and scope, the importance of a defined security policy for all users increases drastically. Some things to include in a security policy are: identification and authentication policies, password policies, acceptable use policies, remote access policies, and incident handling procedures.

When a security policy is developed, it is necessary that all users of the network support and follow the security policy in order for it to be effective.

Refer to
Figure
in online course

A security policy should be the central point for how a network is secured, monitored, tested and improved upon. Security procedures implement security policies. Procedures define configuration, login, audit, and maintenance processes for hosts and network devices. They include the use of both preventative measures to reduce risk, as well as active measure for how to handle known security threats. Security Procedures can range from simple, inexpensive tasks such as maintaining up-to-date software releases, to complex implementations of firewalls and intrusion detection systems.

Some of the security tools and applications used in securing a network include:

- Software patches and updates
- Virus protection
- Spyware protection
- Spam blockers
- Popup blockers
- Firewalls

8.3.2 Updates and Patches

Refer to
Figure
in online course

Patches and Updates

One of the most common methods that a *hacker* uses to gain access to hosts and/or networks is through software vulnerabilities. It is important to keep software applications up-to-date with the latest security patches and updates to help deter threats. A patch is a small piece of code that fixes a specific problem. An update, on the other hand, may include additional functionality to the software package as well as patches for specific issues.

OS (operating system, such as *Linux*, Windows, etc.) and application vendors continuously provide updates and security patches that can correct known vulnerabilities in the software. In addition, vendors often release collections of patches and updates called service packs. Fortunately, many operating systems offer an automatic update feature that allows OS and applications updates to be automatically downloaded and installed on a host.

8.3.3 Anti-virus Software

Refer to
Figure
in online course

Antivirus Software (Detecting a virus)

Even when the OS and applications have all the current patches and updates, they may still be susceptible to attack. Any device that is connected to a network is susceptible to viruses, worms and Trojan horses. These may be used to corrupt OS code, affect computer performance, alter applications, and destroy data.

Some of the signs that a virus, worm or Trojan horse may be present include:

- Computer starts acting abnormally
- Program does not respond to mouse and keystrokes
- Programs starting or shutting down on their own
- Email program begins sending out large quantities of email
- CPU usage is very high
- There are unidentifiable, or a large number of processes running
- Computer slows down significantly or crashes

Refer to
Figure
in online course

Anti-virus Software

Anti-virus software can be used as both a preventative tool and as a reactive tool. It prevents infection and detects, and removes, viruses, worms and Trojan horses. Anti-virus software should be installed on all computers connected to the network. There are many Anti-virus programs available.

Some of the features that can be included in Anti-virus programs are:

- *Email checking* - Scans incoming and outgoing emails, and identifies suspicious attachments.
- *Resident dynamic scanning* - Checks executable files and documents when they are accessed.
- *Scheduled scans* - Virus scans can be scheduled to run at regular intervals and check specific drives or the entire computer.
- *Automatic Updates* - Checks for, and downloads, known virus characteristics and patterns. Can be scheduled to check for updates on a regular basis.

Anti-virus software relies on knowledge of the virus to remove it. Therefore, when a virus is identified, it is important to report it or any virus-like behavior to the network administrator. This is normally done by submitting an incident report according to the company's network security policy.

Network administrators can also report new instances of threats to the local governmental agency that handle security problems. For example, an agency in the U.S. is: https://forms.us-cert.gov/report/. This agency is responsible for developing counter measures to new virus threats as well as ensuring that those measures are available to the various anti-virus software developers.

8.3.4 Anti-spam

Refer to
Figure
in online course

Spam is not only annoying; it can overload email servers and potentially carry viruses and other security threats. Additionally, Spammers take control of a host by planting code on it in the form of a virus or a Trojan horse. The host is then used to send spam mail without the user's knowledge. A computer infected this way is known as a Spam mill.

Anti-spam software protects hosts by identifying spam and performing an action, such as placing it into a junk folder or deleting it. It can be loaded on a machine locally, but can also be loaded on email servers. In addition, many ISPs offer spam filters. Anti-spam software does not recognize all spam, so it is important to open email carefully. It may also accidentally identify wanted email as spam and treat it as such.

Refer to
Figure
in online course

In addition to using spam blockers, other preventative actions to prevent the spread of spam include:

- Apply OS and application updates when available.

- Run an Antivirus program regularly and keep it up to date.

- Do not forward suspect emails.

- Do not open email attachments, especially from people you do not know.

- Set up rules in your email to delete spam that by-pass the anti-spam software.

- Identify sources of spam and report it to a network administrator so it can be blocked.

- Report incidents to the governmental agency that deals with abuse by spam.

One of the most common types of spam forwarded is a virus warning. While some virus warnings sent via email are true, a large amount of them are hoaxes and do not really exist. This type of spam can create problems because people warn others of the impending disaster and so flood the email system. In addition, network administrators may overreact and waste time investigating a problem that does not exist. Finally, many of these emails can actually contribute to the spread of viruses, worms and Trojan horses. Before forwarding virus warning emails, check to see if the virus is a hoax at a trusted source such as: http://vil.mcafee.com/hoax.asp or http://www.virusbtn.com/resources/hoaxes/index

8.3.5 Anti-spyware

Refer to
Figure
in online course

Anti-Spyware and Adware

Spyware and *adware* can also cause virus-like symptoms. In addition to collecting unauthorized information, they can use important computer resources and affect performance. Anti-spyware software detects and deletes spyware applications, as well as prevents future installations from occurring. Many Anti-Spyware applications also include detection and deletion of cookies and adware. Some Anti-virus packages include Anti-Spyware functionality.

Popup Blockers

Popup stopper software can be installed to prevent popups and pop-unders. Many web browsers include a *popup blocker* feature by default. Note that some programs and web pages create necessary and desirable popups. Most popup blockers offer an override feature for this purpose.

Refer to
Interactive Graphic
in online course.

Activity

Identify the purpose of each security tool.

Drag the security tool to the appropriate definition

8.4   Using Firewalls

8.4.1   What is a Firewall?

Refer to
Figure
in online course

In addition to protecting individual computers and servers attached to the network, it is important to control traffic traveling to and from the network.

A Firewall is one of the most effective security tools available for protecting internal network users from external threats. A firewall resides between two or more networks and controls the traffic between them as well as helps prevent unauthorized access. Firewall products use various techniques for determining what is permitted or denied access to a network.

- *Packet Filtering* - Prevents or allows access based on IP or MAC addresses.

- *Application Filtering* - Prevents or allows access to specific application types based on port numbers.

- *URL* Filtering - Prevents or allows access to websites based on specific URLs or keywords.

- *Stateful Packet Inspection (SPI)* - Incoming packets must be legitimate responses to requests from internal hosts. Unsolicited packets are blocked unless permitted specifically. SPI can also include the capability to recognize and filter out specific types of attacks such as DoS.

Firewall products may support one or more of these filtering capabilities. Additionally, Firewalls often perform Network Address Translation (NAT). NAT translates an internal address or group of addresses into an outside, public address that is sent across the network. This allows internal IP addresses to be concealed from outside users.

Refer to
Figure
in online course

Firewall products come packaged in various forms:

- *Appliance-based firewalls* - An appliance-based firewall is a firewall that is built-in to a dedicated hardware device known as a security appliance.

- *Server-based firewalls* - A server-based firewall consists of a firewall application that runs on a network operating system (NOS) such as *UNIX*, Windows or Novell.

- *Integrated Firewalls* - An integrated firewall is implemented by adding firewall functionality to an existing device, such as a router.

- *Personal firewalls* - Personal firewalls reside on host computers and are not designed for LAN implementations. They may be available by default from the OS or may be installed from an outside vendor.

8.4.2   Using a Firewall

Refer to
Figure
in online course

By placing the firewall between the internal network (*intranet*) and the Internet as a border device, all traffic to and from the Internet can be monitored and controlled. This creates a clear line of defense between the internal and external network. However, there may be some external customers that require access to internal resources. A *demilitarized zone (DMZ)* can be configured to accomplish this.

The term demilitarized zone is borrowed from the military, where a DMZ is a designated area between two powers where military activity is not permitted. In computer networking, a DMZ refers to an area of the network that is accessible to both internal and external users. It is more secure than the external network but not as secure as the internal network. It is created by one or more firewalls to separate the internal, DMZ and external networks. Web servers for public access are frequently placed in a DMZ.

Single firewall configuration

Refer to
Figure
in online course

A single firewall has three areas, one for the external network, the internal network, and the DMZ. All traffic is sent to the firewall from the external network. The firewall is then required to monitor the traffic and determine what traffic should be passed to the DMZ, what traffic should be passed internally, and what should be denied altogether.

Two firewall configuration

In a two firewall configuration, there is an internal and external firewall with the DMZ located between them. The external firewall is less restrictive and allows Internet user access to the services in the DMZ as well as allowing a traffic that any internal user requested to pass through. The internal firewall is more restrictive and protects the internal network from unauthorized access.

A single firewall configuration is appropriate for smaller, less congested networks. However, a single firewall configuration does have a single point of failure and can be overloaded. A two-firewall configuration is more appropriate for larger, more complex networks that handle a lot more traffic.

Refer to
Figure
in online course

Many home network devices, such as integrated routers, frequently include multi-function firewall software. This firewall typically provides Network Address Translation (NAT), Stateful Packet Inspection (SPI) and IP, Application and web site filtering capabilities. They also support DMZ capabilities.

With the integrated router, a simple DMZ can be set up that allows an internal server to be accessible by outside hosts. To accomplish this, the server requires a *static IP address* that must be specified in the DMZ configuration. The integrated router isolates traffic destined to the IP address specified. This traffic is then forwarded only to the switch port where the server is connected. All other hosts are still protected by the firewall.

When the DMZ is enabled, in its simplest form, outside hosts can access all ports on the server, such as 80 (HTTP), 21 (FTP), and 110 (Email POP3), etc.

A more restrictive DMZ can be set up using the port forwarding capability. With port forwarding, ports that should be accessible on the server are specified. In this case, only traffic destined for those port(s) is allowed, all other traffic is excluded.

The wireless access point within the integrated router is considered part of the internal network. It is important to realize that if the wireless access point is unsecured, anyone who connects to it is within the protected part of the internal network and is behind the firewall. Hackers can use this to gain access to the internal network and completely bypass any security.

Refer to
Lab Activity
for this chapter

Lab Activity

Configure firewall settings using the Linksys GUI interface and use it to create a DMZ.

8.4.3 Vulnerability Analysis

Refer to
Figure
in online course

There are many vulnerability analysis tools for testing host and network security. These are known as security scanners, and can help identify areas where attacks might occur and offer guidance on steps that can be taken. While the capabilities of the vulnerability analysis tools can vary based on manufacturer, some of the more common features include determining:

■ Number of hosts available on a network

■ The services hosts are offering

- The operating system and versions on the hosts

- Packet filters and firewalls in use

Lab Activity

Refer to
Lab Activity
for this chapter

Research, download and install a Security Vulnerability tester and use it to determine weaknesses in a host and the network.

8.4.4 Best Practices

Refer to
Figure
in online course

There are several recommended practices to help mitigate the risks they pose, including:

- Define security policies

- Physically secure servers and network equipment

- Set login and file access permissions

- Update OS and applications

- Change permissive default settings

- Run anti-virus and anti-spyware

- Update antivirus software files

- Activate browser tools - Popup stoppers, anti-phishing, plug-in monitors

- Use a firewall

The first step towards securing a network is to understand how traffic moves across the network and the different threats and vulnerabilities that exist. Once security measures are implemented, a truly secure network needs to be monitored constantly. Security procedures and tools need to be reviewed in order to stay ahead of evolving threats.

Summary

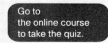

Quiz

Take the chapter quiz to check your knowledge.

Your Chapter Notes

CHAPTER 9

Troubleshooting Your Network

Introduction

Refer to
Figure
in online course

9.1 Troubleshooting Process

9.1.1 Troubleshooting

Refer to
Figure
in online course

Troubleshooting is the process of identifying, locating and correcting problems that occur. Experienced individuals often rely on instinct to troubleshoot. However, there are structured techniques that can be used to determine the most probable cause and solution.

When troubleshooting, proper documentation must be maintained. This documentation should include as much information as possible about:

- The problem encountered
- Steps taken to determine the cause of the problem
- Steps to correct the problem and ensure that it will not reoccur

Document all steps taken in troubleshooting, even the ones that did not solve the issue. This documentation becomes a valuable reference should the same or similar problem occur again.

9.1.2 Gathering Information

Refer to
Figure
in online course

When a problem is reported, verify it and determine the extent. Once the problem is confirmed, the first step in troubleshooting is to gather information.

Gathering information

One of the first ways to gather information is to question the individual who reported the problem as well as any other affected users. Questions can include: end user experiences, observed symptoms, error messages and information about recent configuration changes to devices or applications.

Next, collect information about any equipment that may be affected. This can be gathered from documentation. A copy of all log files and a listing of any recent changes made to equipment configurations is also necessary. Other information on the equipment includes the manufacturer, make and model of devices affected, as well as ownership and warranty information. The version of any firmware or software on the device is also important because there may be compatibility problems with particular hardware platforms.

Information about the network can also be gathered using network monitoring tools. Network monitoring tools are complex applications often used on large networks to continually gather information about the state of the network and network devices. These tools may not be available for smaller networks.

Once all necessary information is gathered start the troubleshooting process.

9.1.3 Approaches to Troubleshooting

Refer to
Figure
in online course

There are several different structured troubleshooting techniques available, including:

- Top-down
- Bottom-up
- Divide-and-conquer

All of these structured approaches assume a layered concept of networking. An example of a layered approach is the OSI model, in which every function of communication is broken down into seven distinct layers. Using this model, a troubleshooter can verify all functionality at each layer until the problem is located and isolated.

Top-down starts with the *application layer* and works down. It looks at the problem from the point of view of the user and the application. Is it just one application that is not functioning, or do all applications fail? For example, can the user access various web pages on the Internet, but not email? Do other workstations have similar issues?

Bottom-up starts with the physical layer and works up. The physical layer is concerned with hardware and wire connections. Have cables been pulled out of their sockets? If the equipment has indicator lights, are they on or off?

Divide-and-Conquer typically begins troubleshooting at one of the middle layers and works up or down from there. For example, the troubleshooter may begin at the network layer, by verifying IP configuration information.

The structure of these approaches makes them ideally suited for the novice troubleshooter. More experienced individuals often bypass structured approaches and rely on instinct and experience. They may use less structured techniques such as trial and error or substitution.

Refer to
Figure
in online course

Trial and Error

Trial and error relies on individual knowledge to determine the most probable cause of a problem. A troubleshooter makes an educated guess on the most likely solution based on past experience and knowledge of the network structure. Once the solution is implemented, if it does not work, the troubleshooter uses this information to help determine the next most likely cause. This process is repeated until the problem is isolated and solved.

While the trial and error approach has the potential to be extremely fast, it relies on the abilities and experiences of the troubleshooter and can result in incorrect assumptions and overlooking simple solutions.

Substitution

With this technique the problem is assumed to be caused by a specific hardware component or a configuration file. The defective part or code is replaced by a known good device or file. While not necessarily locating the problem, this technique can save time and quickly restore network functionality. This relies on the availability of substitute parts, components, and backup configuration files which can be very expensive to maintain.

An example of a substitution technique is when an ISP replaces a possible broken device rather than send a technician out to troubleshoot and locate a specific issue. This technique is also often used for inexpensive parts such as replacing network interface cards and patch cables.

Refer to Interactive Graphic in online course.

Activity

Identify the troubleshooting technique used in a given scenario.

Select the troubleshooting approach being described in the scenario.

9.2 Troubleshooting Issues

9.2.1 Detecting Physical Problems

Refer to Figure in online course

A large proportion of networking problems are related to physical components or problems with the physical layer.

Physical problems are concerned mainly with the hardware aspects of computers and networking devices and the cables that interconnect them. Physical problems do not consider the logical (software) configuration of devices.

Physical problems can occur in both wired and wireless networks. One of the best detection methods for physical problems is the use of the senses - vision, smell, touch and hearing.

9.2.2 Software Utilities for Troubleshooting Connectivity

Refer to Figure in online course

A number of software utility programs are available that can help identify network problems. Most of these utilities are provided by the operating system as command line interface (CLI) commands. The syntax for the commands may vary between operating systems.

Some of the available utilities include:

- **`ipconfig`** - Displays IP configuration information
- **`ping`** - Tests connections to other IP hosts
- **`tracert`** - Displays route taken to destination
- `netstat` - Displays network connections
- **`nslookup`** - Directly queries the name server for information on a destination domain

9.2.3 Troubleshooting Using Ipconfig

Refer to Figure in online course

Ipconfig

Ipconfig is used to display the current IP configuration information for a host. Issuing this command from the command prompt will display the basic configuration information including: IP address, subnet mask and default gateway.

Ipconfig /all

The command ipconfig /all displays additional information including the MAC address, IP addresses of the default gateway and the DNS servers. It also indicates if DHCP is enabled, the DHCP server address and lease information.

How can this utility assist in the troubleshooting process? Without an appropriate IP configuration, a host can not participate in communications on a network. If the host does not know the location of the DNS servers it cannot translate names into IP addresses.

Ipconfig /release and **ipconfig /renew**

If IP addressing information is assigned dynamically, the command ipconfig /release will release the current DHCP bindings. Ipconfig /renew will request fresh configuration information from the DHCP server. A host may contain faulty or outdated IP configuration information and a simple renewal of this information is all that is required to regain connectivity.

If after releasing the IP configuration, the host is unable to obtain fresh information from the DHCP server, it could be that there is no network connectivity. Verify that the NIC has an illuminated link light, indicating that it has a physical connection to the network. If this does not solve the problem, it may be an issue with the DHCP server or network connections to the DCHP server.

Refer to **Packet Tracer Activity** for this chapter

Packet Tracer Activity

Use the `ipconfig` command to examine IP configuration information on a host.

9.2.4 Troubleshooting Using Ping

Refer to **Figure** in online course

Ping

If the IP configuration appears to be correctly configured on the local host, next, test network connectivity by using ping. Ping is used to test if a destination host is reachable. The ping command can be followed by either an IP address or the name of a destination host, as for example:

`ping 192.168.7.5`

pingwww.cisco.com

When a ping is sent to an IP address, a packet known as an echo request is sent across the network to the IP address specified. If the destination host receives the echo request, it responds with a packet known as an echo reply. If the source receives the echo reply, connectivity is verified.

If a ping is sent to a name, such as www.cisco.com, a packet is first sent to a DNS server to resolve the name to an IP address. Once the IP address is obtained, the echo request is forwarded to the IP address and the process proceeds. If a ping to the IP address succeeds, but a ping to the name does not, there is most likely a problem with DNS.

Refer to **Figure** in online course

If pings to both the name and IP address are successful, but the user is still unable to access the application, then the problem most likely resides in the application on the destination host. For example, it may be that the requested service is not running.

If neither ping is successful, then network connectivity along the path to the destination is most likely the problem. If this occurs, it is common practice to ping the default gateway. If the ping to the default gateway is successful, the problem is not local. If the ping to the default gateway fails, the problem resides on the local network.

The basic ping command usually issues four echoes and waits for the replies to each one. It can, however, be modified to increase its usefulness. The Options listed in the graphic display additional features available.

Refer to **Packet Tracer Activity** for this chapter

Packet Tracer Activity

Use `ping` to examine end-to-end connectivity between hosts.

9.2.5 Troubleshooting Using Tracert

Refer to **Figure** in online course

Tracert

The ping utility can verify end-to-end connectivity. However, if a problem exists and the device cannot ping the destination, the ping utility does not indicate where the connection was actually dropped. To accomplish this, another utility known as tracert must be used.

The Tracert utility provides connectivity information about the path a packet takes to reach the destination and about every router (hop) along the way. It also indicates how long a packet takes to get from the source to each hop and back (round trip time). Tracert can help identify where a packet may have been lost or delayed due to bottlenecks or slowdowns in the network.

The basic tracert utility will only allow up to 30 hops between a source and destination device before it assumes that the destination is unreachable. This number is adjustable by using the -h parameter. Other modifiers, displayed as Options in the graphic, are also available.

9.2.6 Troubleshooting Using Netstat

Refer to **Figure** in online course

Netstat

Sometimes it is necessary to know which active TCP connections are open and running on a networked host. Netstat is an important network utility that can be used to verify those connections. Netstat lists the protocol in use, the local address and port number, the foreign address and port number, and the state of the connection.

Unexplained TCP connections can pose a major security threat. This is because they can indicate that something or someone is connected to the local host. Additionally, unnecessary TCP connections can consume valuable system resources thus slowing down the host's performance. Netstat should be used to examine the open connections on a host when performance appears to be compromised.

Many useful Options are available for the `netstat` command.

9.2.7 Troubleshooting Using Nslookup

Refer to **Figure** in online course

Nslookup

When accessing applications or services across the network, individuals usually rely on the DNS name instead of the IP address. When a request is sent to that name, the host must first contact the DNS server to resolve the name to the corresponding IP. The host then uses IP to package the information for delivery.

The nslookup utility allows an end-user to look up information about a particular DNS name in the DNS server. When the nslookup command is issued, the information returned includes the IP address of the DNS server being used as well as the IP address associated with the specified DNS name. Nslookup is often used as a troubleshooting tool for determining if the DNS server is performing name resolution as expected.

Refer to **Lab Activity** for this chapter

Lab Activity

Use various troubleshooting utilities to diagnose and correct connectivity problems.

9.3 Common Issues

9.3.1 Connectivity Issues

Refer to
Figure
in online course

Connectivity problems occur on wireless networks, wired networks and networks that use both. When troubleshooting a network with both wired and wireless connections, it is often best to troubleshoot using a divide-and -conquer technique to isolate the problem to either the wired or wireless network. The easiest way to determine if the problem is with the wired or the wireless network is to:

Step 1.   Ping from a wireless client to the default gateway - this verifies if the wireless client is connecting as expected.

Step 2.   Ping from a wired client to the default gateway - this verifies if the wired client is connecting as expected.

Step 3.   Ping from the wireless client to a wired client - this verifies if the integrated router is functioning as expected.

Once the problem is isolated it can be corrected.

9.3.2 LED Indicators

Refer to
Figure
in online course

Regardless of whether the fault is present on the wireless or wired network, one of the first steps of troubleshooting should be to examine the LEDs, which indicate the current state or activity of a piece of equipment or connection. LEDs may change color or flash to convey information. The exact configuration and meaning of LEDs varies between manufacturers and devices.

Three types of LEDs are commonly found on devices - power, status and activity. On some devices a single LED may convey multiple pieces of information depending on the current status of the device. It is important to check the equipment documentation for the exact meaning of all indicators but some commonality does exist.

Inactive LEDs may be an indication of a device failure, port failure, or cabling issues. It is possible that the device is non-functional due to faulty hardware. The port itself might also have become faulty due to hardware or improperly configured software. Regardless of whether the network is wired or wireless, verify that the device and ports are up and functional before spending large amounts of time trying to troubleshoot other issues.

9.3.3 Connectivity Problems

Refer to
Figure
in online course

Wired host cannot connect to the integrated router

If the wired client is unable to connect to the integrated router, one of the first things to check is the physical connectivity and cabling. Cabling is the central nervous system of wired networks and one of the most common issues when experiencing inactivity.

There are several issues to watch for in cabling:

Step 1.   Be sure to use the correct type of cable. Two types of UTP cables are commonly encountered in networking: Straight-through cables and Cross-over cables. Using the wrong type of cable may prevent connectivity.

Step 2.   Improper cable termination is one of the main problems encountered in networks. To avoid this, cables should be terminated according to standards.

■ Terminate cables via 568A or 568B termination standard

■ Avoid untwisting too much cable during termination

■ Crimp connectors on the cable jacket to provide strain relief

Step 3.   Maximum cable run lengths exist based on characteristics of the different cables. Exceeding these run lengths can have a serious negative impact on network performance.

Step 4.   If connectivity is a problem, verify that the correct ports are being used between the networking devices.

Step 5.   Protect cables and connectors from physical damage. Support cables to prevent strain on connectors and run cable through areas that will not be in the way.

Refer to
Lab Activity
for this chapter

Lab Activity

Investigate and correct various connectivity problems related to cabling issues.

9.3.4 Troubleshooting Radio Problems in a WLAN

Refer to
Figure
in online course

Wireless host cannot connect to the AP

If the wireless client is unable to connect to the AP, it may be because of wireless connectivity problems. Wireless communications rely on radio frequency signals (RF) to carry data. Many factors can affect our ability to connect hosts using RF.

Step 1.   Not all wireless standards are compatible. The 802.11a (5 GHz band) is not compatible with the 802.11b/g/n standards (2.4 GHz band). Within the 2.4 GHz band, each standard uses different technology. Unless specifically configured, equipment that conforms to one standard may not function with that conforming to another.

Step 2.   Each wireless conversation must occur on a separate, non-overlapping channel. Some AP devices can be configured to select the least congested or highest throughput channel. Although automatic settings work, manual setting of the AP channel provides greater control and may be necessary in some environments.

Step 3.   The strength of an RF signal decreases with distance. If the signal strength is too low, devices will be unable to reliably associate and move data. The signal may be dropped. The NIC client utility can be used to display the signal strength and connection quality.

Step 4.   RF signals are susceptible to interference from outside sources, including other devices functioning on the same frequency. A site survey should be used to detect for this.

Step 5.   APs share the available bandwidth between devices. As more devices associate with the AP, the bandwidth for each individual device will decrease causing network performance problems. The solution is to reduce the number of wireless clients using each channel.

Refer to
Interactive Graphic
in online course.

Activity

Construct a Basic Service Set (BSS) capable of supporting multiple wireless clients.

Drag the APs and wireless clients into the BSS. Click each to set the proper channel for communication.

9.3.5 Troubleshooting Association & Authentication on a WLAN

Refer to
Figure
in online course

Wireless configuration problems

Modern WLANs incorporate various technologies to help secure the data on the WLAN: incorrect configuration of any of these can prevent communication. Some of the most common settings that are configured incorrectly include: the SSID, authentication and encryption.

Step 1.   The SSID is a case-sensitive, alpha-numeric string up to 32-characters. It must match on both the AP and client. If the SSID is broadcast and detected, this is not an issue. If the SSID is not broadcast, it must be manually entered onto the client. If the client is configured with the wrong SSID, it will not associate with the AP. Additionally, if another AP is present that is broadcasting the SSID, the client may automatically associate to it.

Step 2.   On most APs open authentication is configured by default, allowing all devices to connect. If a more secure form of authentication is configured, a key is necessary. Both the client and the AP must be configured with the same key. If the keys do not match, authentication will fail and the devices will not associate.

Encryption is the process of altering the data so that it is not usable by anyone without the proper encryption key. If encryption is enabled, the same encryption key must be configured on both the AP and the client. If the client associates with the AP but can not send or receive data, the encryption key may be the issue.

Refer to **Packet Tracer Activity** for this chapter

Packet Tracer Activity

Given a scenario, determine the reason why a wireless STA is unable to connect to a WLAN and correct the problem.

9.3.6 DHCP Issues

Refer to **Figure** in online course

Determining if your computer is obtaining the correct IP address

If the physical connection to the wired or wireless host appears to be connecting as expected, then check the IP configuration of the client.

The IP configuration can have a major impact on the ability for a host to connect to the network. An integrated router, such as the Linksys wireless router, acts as a DHCP server for local wired and wireless clients and provides IP configuration, including the IP address, subnet mask, default gateway, and possibly even IP addresses of DNS servers. The DHCP server binds the IP address to a client's MAC address and stores that information in a client table. On the home Linksys wireless router, this table can be examined through the Status | Local Network page in the GUI.

The client table information should match the local host information, which can be obtained from the `ipconfig /all` command. Additionally, the IP address on the client must be on the same network as the LAN interface of the Linksys device. The LAN interface of the Linksys device should be set as the default gateway. If the client configuration information does not agree with information in the client table, the address should be released (`ipconfig /release`) and renewed (`ipconfig /renew`) to form a new binding.

If both the wired and wireless clients are obtaining the correct IP configuration, and can connect to the Linksys device, but are unable to ping each other, the problem is most likely occurring on the Linksys device. Check all configurations on the Linksys device to ensure no security restrictions could be causing the issue.

Refer to **Interactive Graphic** in online course.

Activity

Sort the problem according to which part of the network they can be associated with, wired, wireless or both.

Drag each problem into the wired, wireless or both categories.

9.3.7 Troubleshooting the ISR to ISP Connection

Refer to **Figure** in online course

Wired and wireless hosts can connect to each other, but not to the Internet

If hosts on the wired and wireless local network can connect to the integrated router and with other hosts on the local network, but not to the Internet, the problem may be in the connection between the integrated router and the ISP.

There are many ways to verify connectivity between the integrated router and the ISP. Using the GUI, one way to check connectivity is to examine the router status page. It should show the IP address assigned by the ISP and should indicate if the connection is established.

If this page shows no connection, the integrated router may not be connected. Check all physical connections and LED indicators. If the DSL or Cable modem is a separate device, check those connections and indicators as well. If the ISP requires a login name or password, check that they are configured to match those given by the ISP. Using the GUI, password configurations can normally be located on the Sctup configuration page. Next, try to re-establish connectivity by clicking the **Connect**, or **IP address renew**, button on the status page. If the integrated router will still not connect, contact the ISP to see if the issue is occurring from their end.

If the status page shows that the connection is up, but a ping to an Internet site fails, it may be that the individual site is down. Try pinging another site to see if that is successful. If not, check for security measures that are enabled that may be creating the issue, such as port filtering.

9.4 Troubleshooting and the Helpdesk

9.4.1 Documentation

Refer to **Figure** in online course

Network documentation is an important part of any troubleshooting process. Network documentation should include a normal or baseline measurement of network performance against which potential problems can be judged.

The performance baseline can include the types of traffic normally expected, as well as the volume of traffic to and from servers and network devices. The baseline should be documented just after the network is installed, when it is running optimally. Baseline performance should be re-established after any major changes to the network are implemented.

Additionally, documentation such as topology maps, network diagrams and addressing schemes can provide valuable information when a troubleshooter is trying to understand the physical layout of the network and the logical flow of information.

When troubleshooting, documentation should be maintained during the troubleshooting process. This documentation can be a valuable reference and can be used when future issues arise. Good troubleshooting documentation should include:

- Initial problem
- Steps taken to isolate the problem
- Results of all steps taken, both successful and unsuccessful
- Final determined cause of the problem

- Final problem resolution

- Preventative measures

9.4.2 Using Outside Sources for Help

Refer to
Figure
in online course

If, during the troubleshooting process, the troubleshooter is unable to determine the problem and its resolution, it might be necessary to obtain assistance from outside sources. Some of the most common sources for help include:

- Previously kept documentation

- Online FAQs (Frequently Asked Questions)

- Colleagues and other network professionals

- Internet forums

9.4.3 Using the Helpdesk

Refer to
Figure
in online course

The helpdesk is the end-user's first stop for assistance. The helpdesk is a group of individuals with the knowledge and tools required to help diagnose and correct common problems. It provides assistance for the end-user to determine if a problem exists, the nature of the problem, and the solution.

Many companies and ISPs establish helpdesks to assist their users with networking problems. Most large IT companies run helpdesks for their individual products or technologies. For example, Cisco Systems offers helpdesk assistance for problems integrating Cisco equipment into a network, or problems that may occur after installation.

There are many ways to contact a helpdesk, including email, live chat, and phone. While email is good for non-urgent problems, phone or live chat is better for network emergencies. This is especially important in organizations such as banks where small amounts of downtime can cost large amounts of money.

If necessary, the helpdesk can take control of a local host through remote access software. This allows helpdesk technicians to run diagnostic programs and interact with the host and network without having to physically travel to a job site. This greatly reduces the wait time for problem resolution and allows the helpdesk to assist more users.

Refer to
Figure
in online course

As an end user, it is important to give the help desk as much information as possible. The helpdesk will require information on any service or support plans that are in place along with specific details of the affected equipment. This can include make, model and serial number along with the version of firmware or operating system running on the device. They may also require the IP and MAC address of the malfunctioning device. The helpdesk will require information specific to the problem including:

- Symptoms encountered

- Who encountered the problem

- When the problem manifests

- Steps taken to identify the problem

- Results of steps taken

If this is a follow-up call, be prepared to provide the date and time of the previous call, the ticket number, and name of the technician. Be at the affected equipment, and be prepared to provide the helpdesk staff with access to the equipment if requested.

Refer to
Figure
in online course

A helpdesk is generally organized in a series of levels of experience and knowledge. If the first-level helpdesk staff is unable to solve the problem they may escalate the problem to a higher level. Higher level staff are generally more knowledgeable and have access to resources and tools that the first-level helpdesk does not.

Record all information regarding the interaction with the helpdesk, such as:

- Time/date of call
- Name/ID of technician
- Problem reported
- Course of action taken
- Resolution/escalation
- Next steps (follow-up)

By working together with the helpdesk, most problems can be resolved quickly and easily. Once resolved, be sure to update all documentation accordingly for future reference.

Summary

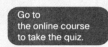

Go to
the online course
to take the quiz.

Quiz

Take the chapter quiz to check your knowledge.

Your Chapter Notes

CHAPTER 10

Course Summary

10.0 Putting It All Together

Summary

Refer to **Figure** in online course

Summary Activity

Throughout this course, you have learned about computer hardware and software, wired and wireless networking components, protocols and applications, and techniques for securing a network.

In this summary activity, use the knowledge you have gained to plan and implement a technical solution for a small business. Your solution should be based on the needs and requirements of the business environment.

Click the icon to begin.

Your Chapter Notes

802.11a

IEEE standard for wireless LANs that operates in 5 GHz band, uses 52-subcarrier orthogonal frequency-division multiplexing (OFDM) with a maximum raw data rate of 54 Mbps,

802.11b

The first widely accepted wireless networking standard. Since it operates in the 2.4 GHz band, other devices that operate in the same band can cause interference.

802.11g

An extension of the 802.11 standard. 802.11g applies to wireless LANs and provides up to 54 Mbps. Since it operates in the 2.4 GHz band, other devices that operate in the same band can cause interference.

802.11n

A proposed new extension to the 802.11 standard. 802.11n applies to wireless LANs and provides up to 540 Mbps in the 2.4 or 5 GHz band.

access layer

The first point of entry into the network for all hosts. The access layer provides a physical connection to the network as well as authentication and traffic control. A component of the Cisco 3-layer network design approach that also includes a distribution layer and a core layer. The access layer provides entry to the network closest to end users.

access method

A set of rules used by LAN hardware to direct traffic on the network. It determines which host or device uses the LAN next.

access point

Wireless LAN transmitter/receiver that acts as a connection between wireless clients and wired networks.

ACK

Acknowledgement. A transmission control character (or a transmission frame) that confirms a transmitted message was received uncorrupted or without errors or that the receiving station is ready to accept transmissions.

adware

A software program that once installed, automatically displays advertising material on a computer.

AES

Advanced Encryption Standard. A symmetric 128-bit block cipher that replaces DES as the U.S. government's cryptographic standard. The algorithm must be used with key sizes of 128 bits, 192 bits, or 256 bits, depending on the application security requirement.

AGP

Accelerated Graphics Port. Dedicated high-speed bus that supports the high demands of graphical software. This slot is reserved for video cards only.

AIM

AOL Instant Messenger. Instant message service that supports text chat, photo sharing, online gaming, and PC to PC voice using OSCAR instant message protocol and the TOC protocol.

AIX

Advanced Interactive eXecutive. An operating system based on UNIX. Recent versions of AIX can support up to 64 central processing units and two terabytes of random access memory. AIX is a proprietary operating system developed by IBM.

Apache web server

A public-domain, open-source web server for UNIX-type systems, Microsoft Windows, Novell NetWare, and other operating systems.

application
A software program designed to perform a specific task or group of tasks.

application layer
Layer seven of the OSI model. It interfaces directly to and performs common application services for the application processes. It also issues requests to the presentation layer (sixth layer).

ASCII
American Standard Code for Information Interchange. 8-bit code for character representation (7 bits plus parity). Each letter of the alphabet is assigned a number from 0 to 127.

asynchronous
Without respect to time. In terms of data transmission, asynchronous means that no clock or timing source is needed to keep both the sender and the receiver synchronized

attenuation
The reduction of signal energy during transmission.

authentication
A process implemented on a network to verify the identity of a user.

Automatic Update
A software update service for Microsoft Windows operating systems located on the Microsoft website. The types of software updates available include critical system component updates, service packs, security fixes, patches, and free upgrades to Windows components. The Automatic Update service automatically detects the type of existing hardware.

backside bus
A bus within the central processing unit (CPU) that connects the that connects the CPU with the L2 cache using a dual-bus architecture. The CPU determines the speed of the backside bus.

backup
A copy of data saved onto storage media for the purpose of restoring the data and computer operations in case of data loss. Types of backup include full, incremental, and differential. A backup should be physically removed from the source data.

baseband
A transmission medium through which digital signals are sent without complicated frequency shifting. In general, only one communication channel is available at any given time. Ethernet is an example of a baseband network.

baseline
A quantitative expression of planned costs, schedules, and technical requirements for a defined project. A baseline is established to describe the "normal" status of network or computer system performance. The status can then be compared with the baseline at any point to measure the variation from the "normal" operation condition.

binary
Digital signals that are typically expressed as 1 or 0.

binary digit
A digit with only one and zero as possible values, 1 = on and 0 = off.

BIOS
Basic Input/Output System. Program stored in a ROM chip in the computer that provides the basic code to control the computer's hardware and to perform diagnostics on it. The BIOS prepares the computer to load the operating system.

bit
The smallest unit of data in a computer. A bit can take the value of either 1 or 0. A bit is the binary format in which data is processed by computers. A bit is also known as a binary digit.

blade
A server component or an individual port card that can be added to a network router or switch for additional connectivity.

Blaster worm
Also known as Lovsan or Lovesan. A DoS worm that spread during August 2003 on computers running the Microsoft operating system Windows 2000/XP.

blog
A web page that serves as a publicly accessible personal journal for an individual.

Bluetooth
Wireless industry standard that uses an unlicensed radio frequency for short-range communication enabling portable devices to communicate over short distances

Blu-ray disc
A high-density optical disc format used to store digital media, such as high-definition video.

boot sector
A sector of a data storage device typically the hard drive that contains code for booting the operating system when starting the computer.

botnet
Refers to any group of bots. Typically a collection of compromised machines that distribute worms, Trojan horses, or backdoor viruses.

bots
Software applications that run simple and repetitive tasks over the Internet.

bottom up
A troubleshooting technique in a layered concept of networking that starts with the physical or lowest layer and works up.

bps
bits per second. A unit of measure used to express data transfer rate of bits.

broadcast
A method for sending data packets to all devices on a network. Broadcasts are identified by a broadcast address and rely on routers to keep broadcasts from being sent to other networks.

broadcast domain
Devices within a group that receive the same broadcast frame originating from one of the devices. Broadcast domains are typically bounded by routers because routers do not forward broadcast frames.

broadcast MAC address
Hardware address reserved for frames that are intended for all hosts on a local network segment. Generally, a broadcast address is a MAC destination address of all ones. A broadcast MAC address has the hexadecimal form of FF:FF:FF:FF:FF:FF.

browser
A GUI-based hypertext client application used to access hypertext documents and other services located on innumerable remote servers throughout the WWW and Internet.

brute force attack
A method used to gain access to a network or decrypt a message by systematically entering all possible combinations.

BSS
basic service set. A group of 802.11 devices connected to an access point.

business software
An application designed for use in specific industries or markets.

byte
A unit of measure that describes the size of a data file, the amount of space on a disk or other storage medium, or the amount of data being sent over a network. One byte consists of eight bits of data.

cable modem
Hardware that connects a computer to the cable company network through the same coaxial cabling that feeds cable TV (CATV) signals to a television set.

cache
A data storage area that provides high-speed access for the system.

cache memory
A block of memory in the data storage area that provides the system high-speed access to the data.

CAD
computer-aided design. Application used for creating architectural, electrical, and mechanical design. More complex forms of CAD include solid modeling and parametric modeling, which allow objects to be created with real-world characteristics.

CD
compact disc. Optical storage media for audio and data.

CD-R

compact disc-recordable. Optical media that allows data to be recorded but not modified.

CD-ROM drive

compact disc read only-memory drive. A storage device that reads information that is stored on a compact disc (CD).

CD-RW

compact disc-rewritable. Optical storage media that allows data to be recorded and modified.

cell phone

A portable device that uses wireless communication methods to access a telephone network.

checksum

Method for checking the integrity of transmitted data. A checksum is an integer value computed from a sequence of octets taken through a series of arithmetic operations. The value is recomputed at the receiving end and compared for verification.

chipset

Integrated circuits on a motherboard that enable the CPU to communicate and interact with the other components of the computer.

circuit

The communication path between two or more points that a current or data transmission follows.

Class A

A Class A address has four octets. The first octet is between 1 and 127.The other three octets are used for host addressing. A Class A network can have 16,777,214 hosts.

Class B

A Class B address has four octets. The first octet is between 128 and 191. The first two octets are used to identify the network. The last two octets are for host addressing. A Class B network can have 16,384 networks and 65,534 hosts.

Class C

A Class C address has four octets. The first octet is between 192 and 223. The first three octets identify the network. The last octet is for host addressing. A Class C network can have 2,097,152 networks and 254 hosts.

Class D

A Class D address has four octets. The first octet is between 224 and 239. Class D is used for multicasting.

Class E

A Class E address has four octets. The first octet is between 240 and 255. Class E IP addressing is reserved.

classful addressing

The division of IP addresses into five classes: A, B, C, D, and E. There is a fixed number of networks and hosts associated with each class.

CLI

command line interface. User interface to a computer operating system or application.

client

A network device that participates in a client/server relationship by requesting a service from a server. When a computer is used to access the Internet, the computer is the client and the website is the service requested from the server.

cloud

A symbol that refers to connections in service provider networks.

CMTS

cable modem termination system. A component located at the local cable television company that exchanges digital signals with cable modems on a cable network.

collaboration suite

Application designed to allow the sharing of resources and information within and between organizations.

collision

In Ethernet, the result of two or more devices transmitting simultaneously. The frames from each device impact and are damaged when they meet on the physical media. All computer networks require a mechanism to prevent collisions or to recover quickly when they occur.

collision domain

In Ethernet, the network area where data that is being transmitted simultaneously from two or more computers could collide. Repeaters and hubs propagate collisions; LAN switches, bridges and routers do not.

command.com
Command line interpreter for DOS and 16/32bits versions of Windows (95/98/98 SE/Me). It is the first program run after boot and sets up the system by running the autoexec.bat configuration file.

computer
Electrical machine that can execute a list of instructions and perform calculations based on those instructions.

computer name
Identity of an end-user computer on a wired or wireless network.

connection-oriented
Protocol to establish an end-to end connection before data is sent so that data arrives in the proper sequence.

content filtering
Blocking specific types of web content using content-control or spam blocking solutions.

continuity
The state or quality of being continuous or unbroken. End-to-end continuity tests on cable media can verify that there are no opens or shorts.

controller card
A board, such as a SCSI controller card, that interfaces between the motherboard and a peripheral.

converged network
A network capable of carrying voice, video, and digital data.

convergence
The speed and ability of a group of internetworking devices running a specific routing protocol to agree on the topology of an internetwork after a change in that topology.

Core Layer
One of three basic layers in the hierarchical design of Ethernet networks. The Core Layer is a high-speed backbone layer designed to move large amounts of data quickly. High-speed switches or routers are examples of Core Layer devices.

CPE
customer premises equipment. Terminating equipment, such as terminals, telephones, and modems, supplied by the telephone company, installed at customer sites, and connected to the telephone company network.

CPU
central processing unit. Interprets and processes software instructions and data. Located on the motherboard, the CPU is a chip contained on a single integrated circuit called the microprocessor. The CPU contains two basic components, a control unit and an Arithmetic/Logic Unit (ALU).

cracker
Term used to describe a person who creates or modifies computer software or hardware with the intent to cause harm.

CSMA/CA
carrier sense multiple access with collision avoidance. The basic medium access method for 802.11 wireless networks.

CSMA/CD
carrier sense multiple access with collision detection. The basic access method for Ethernet networks.

CTS
clear to send. Along with request to send (RTS), is used by the 802.11 wireless networking protocol to reduce frame collisions introduced by the hidden terminal problem and exposed node problem.

cuteFTP
Series of FTP client applications providing a simple file transfer interface for Windows-based or Mac-based systems.

data communication
The transfer of encoded information through devices and connections using an electrical transmission system.

data link layer
Layer two of the OSI model. It responds to service requests from the network layer and issues service requests to the physical layer.

data loss

A state where information is unavailable permanently.

database

Organized collection of data that can be easily accessed, managed, indexed, searched, and updated.

datagram

Logical grouping of information sent as a network layer unit over a transmission medium without prior establishment of a virtual circuit. IP datagrams are the primary information units in the Internet.

DDoS

distributed denial of service. An attack by multiple systems on a network that floods the bandwidth or resources of the targeted system, such as a web server, with the purpose to shut it down.

de facto standard

Format, language, or protocol that becomes a standard because it is widely used. De jure standard, in contrast, is one that exists because of approval by an official standards body.

decode

To transform encoded information into information that is readable to a program or a user.

default gateway

The route taken so that a computer on one segment can communicate with a computer on another segment.

demilitarized zone (DMZ)

Describes the area in a network design that is located between the internal network and external network, usually the Internet. It is used for devices accessible to Internet traffic such as the web server, FTP server, SMTP server, and DNS.

desktop computer

Type of computer designed to fit on top of a desk, usually with the monitor on top of the computer to conserve space.

destination host

The computer or other network device that receives data.

DHCP

Dynamic Host Configuration Protocol requests and assigns an IP address, default gateway, and DNS server address to a network host.

DHCP acknowledgement

Dynamic Host Configuration Protocol acknowledgement. DHCP is a software utility that automatically assigns IP addresses in a large network. A server sends a DHCP acknowledgement back to the client when it receives a DHCPREQUEST from the client.

DHCP binding

Dynamic Host Configuration Protocol binding. DHCP is a software utility that automatically assigns IP addresses in a large network. A DHCP binding occurs when an IP address is assigned to a client. The client leases the IP address until the connection is ended.

DHCP client table

Dynamic Host Configuration Protocol client table. DHCP is a software utility that automatically assigns IP addresses in a large network. A DHCP client table is located on the DHCP server and records the assigned IP addresses, MAC addresses, and the amount of time an address is leased.

DHCP discovery

Dynamic Host Configuration Protocol discovery. A packet sent out by the client on a local physical subnet to find available servers.

DHCP offer

Dynamic Host Configuration Protocol offer. A packet sent out by the client requesting an extension on the lease of the IP address. This is done by reserving an IP address for the client and broadcasting a DHCPOFFER message across the network.

DHCP pool

Dynamic Host Configuration Protocol pool. Reserved sets of IP addresses stored on a DHCP server to be dynamically assigned to clients.

DHCP range

Dynamic Host Configuration Protocol range. A contiguous list of IP addresses in a DHCP pool.

DHCP request
Dynamic Host Configuration Protocol request. When the client computer accesses the network, a DHCP packet is sent out by the client requesting a lease if necessary.

DHCP server
Dynamic Host Configuration Protocol (DHCP) is a set of rules for dynamically assigning IP addresses to devices on a network. A DHCP server manages and assigns the IP addresses and ensures that all IP addresses are unique.

dial-up
A form of Internet access using a modem and the public telephone system to dial into an Internet service provider to establish a connection.

digital
A discontinuous signal that changes from one state to another. Also, a data format that uses at least two distinct states to transmit information.

DIP switch
dual in-line package switch. An electrical switch for a dual in-line package used on a printed circuit board.

disk storage
Space on a hard disk or magnetic storage media disk to store data.

distribution system
A network that interconnects multiple BSSs to form an ESS in a wireless LAN. In most part, a distribution system is a wired Ethernet network.

divide and conquer
A troubleshooting technique in a layered concept of networking that can start at any layer and work up or down depending on the outcome.

DNS
Domain Name System. System that provides a way to map friendly host names, or URLs, to IP addresses.

docking station
Device that attaches a laptop to AC power and desktop peripherals.

DoS
denial of service. An attack by a single system on a network that floods the bandwidth or resources of the targeted system, such as a web server, with the purpose to shut it down.

dotted decimal notation
A method of common notation for IP addresses in the form a.b.c.d where each number a represents, in decimal, 1 byte of the 4-byte IP address. Also called dot address.

driver
Specialized software that interprets the output of a device so it can be understood by other devices.

DSL
digital subscriber line. Public network technology that delivers high bandwidth over conventional copper wiring at limited distances. Always-on technology that allows users to connect to the Internet.

DSLAM
digital subscriber line access multiplexer. A device that allows two or more data sources to share a common transmission medium. DSLAM separates DSL phone and data signals and directs them onto networks.

dual core CPU
Two cores inside a single CPU chip. Both cores can be used together to increase speed, or they can be used in two locations at the same time.

DVD
digital video disc. Optical digital disc that stores data. Also called digital versatile disc.

DVD-R
digital video disc-recordable. Technology that allows a DVD to be written to once.

DVD-RW
digital video disk-rewritable. Technology that allows the media to be recorded multiple times.

Dynamic and/or Private Ports
TCP or UDP ports in the range of 49152-65535 that are not used by any defined application.

EAP
Extensible Authentication Protocol. An authentication framework, not a specific authentication mechanism. Most commonly used in wireless LANs, EAP provides common functions and a negotiation of the desired authentication mechanism.

EIA
Electronic Industries Alliance. A trade association that establishes standards for electrical and electronics products.

e-learning
Type of educational instruction using electronic delivery methods such as CD-ROMs, video conferencing, websites, and e-mail.

electromagnetic wave
A self-propagating wave in space with electric and magnetic components classified in order of increasing frequency; radio waves, microwaves, terahertz radiation, infrared radiation, visible light, ultraviolet radiation, x-rays, and gamma rays.

email
Ability for users to communicate over a computer network. The exchange of computer-stored messages by network communication.

EMI
electromagnetic interference. Interference by electromagnetic signals that can cause reduced data integrity and increased error rates on transmission channels.

encryption
The application of a specific algorithm to data so as to alter the appearance of the data making it incomprehensible to those who are not authorized to see the information.

ESD
electrostatic discharge. Discharge of static electricity from one conductor to another conductor of a different potential.

ESS
extended service set. A collection of BSSs that communicate with one another through the distribution system (usually the wired Ethernet port on an access point).

Ethernet cross-over cable
Network cable with transmit and receive wire pairs that are crossed. The cross-over design allows similar devices, such as switch-to-switch, to communicate.

expansion slot
Location in a computer where a PC card can be inserted to add capabilities, such as memory or device support, to the computer.

ext2
second extended file system. File system for the Linux kernel designed to reduce internal fragmentation and mimimize searching by dividing the space into blocks.

ext3
third extended file system. A journalled file system for the Linux operating system.

extranet
Network designed to provide access to specific information or operations of an organization to suppliers, vendors, partners, customers, or other businesses.

FAT
file allocation table. A table of records that the operation system uses to store information about the location of every directory, subdirectory, and file on the hard drive. FAT is stored in track 0 on the hard drive.

FDD
floppy disk drive. Device that spins a magnetically coated floppy disk to read data from and write data to it.

FEXT
far end cross(X) talk. A measurement of crosstalk between pairs of wires used when testing Category 5E or Category 6 cabling. FEXT is measured at the receiving end of the cable.

fiber optics
The transmission of light pulses containing data along glass or plastic wire or fiber. Optical fiber carries more information than conventional copper wire and is less susceptible to electromagnetic interference.

file system
A method used by the operating system to store and organize files. Types of file systems include FAT32, NTFS, HPFS, ext2, and ext3.

firewall
A device or application installed on a network to protect it from unauthorized users and malicious attacks.

firmware
Software embedded in a hardware device typically provided on flash ROMs or as a binary image file that can be uploaded onto existing hardware by a user.

Flash storage
A portable memory hard drive used to store and transport data. Flash storage devices typically have a USB interface and are small, lightweight, removable, and rewritable.

frame
Logical grouping of information sent over a transmission medium as a data link layer unit. Often refers to the header and trailer, used for synchronization and error control, that surround the user data contained in the unit.

frontside bus
A bi-directional bus that carries electronic signals between the central processing unit (CPU) and other devices, such as RAM and hard disks.

FTP
File Transfer Protocol. Application protocol that is part of the TCP/IP protocol stack, used for transferring files between network devices.

full duplex
Data transmission that can go two ways at the same time. An Internet connection using DSL service is an example of full duplex.

gaming device
Powerful computers with higher quality displays used for the purpose of playing video games designed for a particular operating system.

GB
gigabyte. 1,073,741,824, or approximately 1 billion bytes

general use software
An application that is found on most computers home or business computers, such as Microsoft Word.

GHz
gigahertz. Common measurement of a processor equal to one billion cycles per second.

GNU
An operating system that functions using only free software.

GPL
general public license. A license for free and open source operating system software. In contrast to commercial operating system software such as Windows XP, a GPL allows the operating system software, such as Linux and BSD, to be modified. Also called GNU general public license.

GUI
graphical user interface. User-friendly interface that uses graphical images and widgets, along with text, to indicate the information and actions available to a user when interacting with a computer.

hacker
Term used to describe a person who creates or modifies computer software or hardware with the intent to test network security or to cause harm.

half duplex
Data transmission that can go two ways, but not at the same time. Telephones and two-way radios are examples of half duplex.

handheld
Small computing device with input and output capabilities, such as a touch screen or miniature keyboard and display screen.

hard disk
Primary storage medium on a computer.

hardware
Physical electronic components that make up a computer system.

hardware platform
Computer hardware components that use the same unique binary-coded machine language to communicate.

header
Control information placed before data when encapsulating that data for network transmission.

hexadecimal
Using a base 16 number system, s number representation using the digits 0 through 9, with their usual meaning, plus the letters A through F to represent hexadecimal digits with values of 10 to 15. The right-most digit counts ones, the next counts multiples of 16, then $16^2=256$, etc.

horizontal application
Software that can be used across a broad range of the market, such as an office suite.

host
A device that directly participates in network communication. A host can use network resources that are available and/or provide network resources to other hosts on the network.

hot-swappable
The ability to remove, replace, and add peripherals while a system is running.

HPFS
high performance file system. A file system that is able to handle 2TB-volume or 2GB-file disks, and 256-byte file names.

HP-UX
Hewlett-Packard UNIX. A modified version of UNIX used on proprietarty Hewlett-Packard operating systems. HP-UX uses clustering technology, kernal based intrusion detection, and various types of system partitioning.

HTML
HyperText Markup Language. Coding language used to create documents for the World Wide Web.

HTTP
Hypertext Transfer Protocol. A method used to transfer or convey information on the World Wide Web.

HTTP cookie
Small packet of data created by a server and sent to a user's browser and back to the server for authenticating, tracking, and maintaining specific user information, such as site preferences.

hub
A device that serves as the central point of connection for the devices on a LAN.

Hz
hertz. A unit of frequency measurement. It is the rate of change in the state, or cycle, in a sound wave, alternating current, or other cyclical waveform. Hertz is synonymous with cycles per second, and it describes the speed of a computer microprocessor.

IANA
Internet Assigned Numbers Authority. Internet body that oversees global IP address allocation, DNS root zone management, and other Internet protocol assignments.

IBSS
independent basic service set. An 802.11 network comprised of a collection of stations that communicate with each other, but not with a network infrastructure.

identity theft
Personal information stolen for fraudulent purposes.

IDS
Intrusion detection system. A combination of a sensor, console, and central engine in a single device installed on a network to protect against the attacks a conventional firewall can miss.

IE
Internet Explorer. Proprietary web browser developed by Microsoft.

IEEE
Institute of Electrical and Electronics Engineers, A professional organization whose activities include the development of communications and network standards. IEEE LAN standards are the predominant LAN standards today.

IIS

Internet Information Services. Set of Internet-based services for servers using Microsoft Windows.

IMAP

Internet Message Access Protocol. An application layer Internet protocol that allows a local client to access e-mail on a remote server.

impedance

Measurement of the opposition to the flow of alternating current. Impedance is measured in ohms.

infrared

Electromagnetic waves with a frequency range above that of microwaves, but below that of the visible spectrum. LAN systems based on this technology represent an emerging technology.

infrastructure wireless network

Uses spread-spectrum technology, based on radio waves, to enable communication between devices in a limited area, also known as the BSS with at least one wireless station and an AP.

input device

A device that transfers data into the computer. This includes the keyboard, mouse, scanner, and so on.

instant messaging

A real-time text-based method of communication conducted over a network between two or more users.

integrated application

Commonly used applications combined into a single package, such as an office suite.

integrated service router

Device that forwards packets from one network to another based on network layer information. And integrated service router provides secure Internet and intranet access. Normally used in home and small office environments.

interface

1) The connection between two systems or devices. 2) In routing terminology, a network connection. 3) In telephony, a shared boundary defined by common physical interconnection characteristics, signal characteristics, and meanings of interchanged signals. 4) The boundary between adjacent layers of the OSI model.

International Organization for Standardization (IS

Group of representatives from 158 countries, responsible for worldwide industrial and commercial standards.

Internet

Largest global internetwork that connects tens of thousands of networks worldwide.

Internet backbone

Networks with national access points that transport Internet traffic. An Internet service provider uses a router to connect to the backbone.

intranet

Network designed to be accessible only to internal employees of an organization.

IP

Internet Protocol. The network layer protocol in the TCP/IP stack that offers internetwork service. IP provides features for addressing, type-of-service specification, fragmentation and reassembly, and security.

IP address

Internet Protocol address. A 32-bit binary number that is divided into 4 groups of 8 bits, known as octets. IP address is a form of a logical address scheme that provides source and destination addressing and, in conjunction with routing protocols, packet forwarding from one network to another toward a destination.

ipconfig

A DOS command that displays the IP address, subnet mask, and default gateway configured on a PC.

IPS

Intrusion prevention system. An extension of IDS. Based on application content, IPS enhances access control to protect computers from exploitation.

IPtel

Internet Protocol telephony. Method to transmit telephone calls over the Internet using packet-switched technology. Also called voice over IP (VoIP).

IPTV

Internet Protocol television. Method to transmit video using IP packets. Instead of cable or air, IPTV uses the transport protocol of the Internet to deliver video.

IPv4

Internet Protocol version 4. The current Internet Protocol version.

IPv6

Internet Protocol version 6. The next generation of Internet Protocol.

IrDA

infrared data association. Defines protocol standards for the short range exchange of data over infrared light for uses such as PANs.

ISM

industrial, scientific, and medical bands. Radio bands defined by the ITU-R in 5.138 and 5.150 of the Radio Regulations and shared with license-free, error-tolerant communications applications such as wireless LANs and Bluetooth.

ISP

Internet service provider. Company that provides Internet service to home users, such as the local phone or cable company.

IV

initialization vector. A data type that executes an algorithm for a unique encryption stream.

jumper

A pair of prongs that are electrical contact points set into the computer motherboard or an adapter card.

kb

kilobit. 1024, or approximately 1000, bits.

kbps

A measurement of the amount of data that is transferred over a connection such as a network connection. A data transfer rate of 1 kbps is a rate of approximately 1000 bits per second.

kernel

The main module of the operating system that provides the essential services that are needed by applications. The kernel is responsible for managing the system resources and the communication between hardware and software components.

kilobyte

1024, or approximately 1000, bytes. KB

laptop

Small form factor computer designed to be mobile, but operates much the same as a desktop computer. Laptop hardware is proprietary and usually more expensive than desktop hardware.

laser

light amplification by stimulated emission of radiation. Analog transmission device in which a suitable active material is excited by an external stimulus to produce a narrow beam of coherent light that can be modulated into pulses to carry data.

LED

light-emitting diode. Type of computer display that illuminates display screen positions based on the voltages at different grid intersections. Also called a status indicator, the LED indicates whether components inside the computer are on or working.

Linux

Open-source operating system that can be run on various computer platforms.

local application

A software program that is installed and executed on a single computer.

logical address

The network layer address that refers to a logical, rather than a physical, network device.

Lotus Notes

A client-server, collaborative application that provides integrated desktop client option primarily for accessing business e-mail, calendars and applications on an IBM Lotus Domino server.

MAC address
Media Accesss Control address. A standardized data link address that is required for every port or device that connects to a LAN. Other devices in the network use MAC addresses to locate specific ports in the network and to create and update routing tables and data structures. In Ethernet standard, MAC addresses are 6 bytes long.

MAC filtering
Access control method that permits and denies network access based on MAC addresses to specific devices through the use of blacklists and whitelists.

MAC table
Media Access Control table. Table containing MAC addresses of particular ports. A MAC table is used by a switch to identify the destination MAC address.

mainframe
A powerful machine that consists of centralized computers that are usually housed in secure, climate-controlled rooms. End users interface with the computers through dumb terminals.

manual IP address
An IP address that is not obtained automatically, but is manually configured on a computer by the system administrator or user.

Mb
megabit. 1,048,576, or approximately 1 million, bits.

megabyte
MB. 1,048,576, or approximately 1 million, bytes.

megapixel
One million pixels, Image resolution is calculated by multiplying the number of horizontal pixels by the number of vertical pixels.

memory
The physical internal storage medium that holds the data.

memory key
A USB flash drive.

MHz
megahertz . A unit of frequency that equals at one million cycles per second. This is a common measurement of the speed of a processing chip.

Microsoft Exchange Server
A messaging and collaborative software with e-mail, shared calendars and tasks, support for mobile and web-based access to information, and support for large amounts of data storage.

Microsoft Outlook
Information manager in the Microsoft Office suite providing an e-mail application, calendar, task and contact management, note taking, and journal.

modem
modulator-demodulator. Device that converts digital computer signals into a format that is sent and received over an analog telephone line.

Morse code
A coding system that expresses alphabetical characters as pulses of different durations.

motherboard
The main circuit board in a computer. The motherboard connects all the hardware in the computer.

MSN Messenger
Instant messaging client developed and distributed for computers running the Microsoft Windows operating system.

multiboot
An open standard configuration on a partitioned hard drive where each partition has an operating system, files, and configuration settings.

multicast
When a host needs to send messages using a one-to-many pattern, it is referred to as a multicast.

multitasking
The practice of running two or more applications at the same time.

Mutual Authentication
Also known as two-way authentication. Refers to a user or client computer identifying itself to a server and the server identifying itself to the user or client computer so that both are verified.

NAP
network access point. The point at which access providers are interconnected.

NAT
Network address translation. The process of re-writing the source or destination address of IP packets as they pass through a router or firewall so multiple hosts on a private network can access the Internet using a single public IP address.

netstat
A command-line tool that displays incoming and outgoing network connection, routing tables, and various network interface statistics on UNIX and Windows operating systems.

network
A collection of computers, printers, routers, switches, or other devices that are able to communicate with each other over some transmission medium.

network address
The network layer address that refers to a logical, rather than a physical, network device. All network devices must have a unique address. An IP address is an example of a network address.

network application
Software installed on a network server and is accessible to multiple users.

network client
A node or software program that requests services from a server.

network device
A computer, a peripheral, or other related communication equipment attached to a network.

Network layer
Layer three of the OSI model. It responds to service requests from the transport layer and issues service requests to the data link layer.

NEXT
near end cross(X) talk. A measurement of crosstalk between pairs of wires. NEXT is measured near the transmitting end of the cable.

NIC
network interface card. The interface between the computer and the LAN. The NIC is typically inserted into an expansion slot in a computer and connects to the network medium.

NOC
Network Operations Center. An organization responsible for maintaining a network.

nonprofit organization
A business entity that may offer products and service, but not for the purpose of earning a profit.

nonvolatile memory
Memory that retains content, such as configuration information, when a unit is powered off.

NOS
network operating system. An operating system designed to track networks consisting of multiple users and programs. A NOS controls packet traffic and file access, and provides data security. Types of NOS include LAN Manager, Novell NetWare, Sun Solaris, and Windows Server 2003.

nslookup
A command in UNIX and Windows used to find host information in Internet domain name servers.

NTFS
New Technology File System. A Windows file system designed to manage global and enterprise-level operating systems.

octet
A decimal number in the range of 0 to 255 that represents 8 bits.

open authentication
A type of wireless authentication where any and all clients are able to associate regardless of who they are.

open mail relay
An SMTP server configured to allow anyone on the Internet to relay or send e-mail.

OS
operating system. Software program that performs general system tasks, such as controlling RAM, prioritizing the processing, controlling input and output devices, and managing files.

OS/400
Operating system for the AS/400 series of IBM computers. AS/400 is now System i, and OS/400 has been renamed i5/OS.

output device
A device that displays or prints data that is processed by the computer.

packet
A logical grouping of information which includes a header that contains control information and usually user data. Packets are most often used to refer to network layer units of data.

Palm OS
PalmSource Inc. operating system. The operating system for various brands of personal digital assistants.

partition
To divide memory or mass storage into isolated or logical sections. Once a disk is partitioned, each partition will behave like a separate hard drive.

patch panel
Assembly of pin locations and ports that are mounted on a rack or wall bracket in the wiring closet. A patch panel acts like a switchboard that connects to workstations as well as to external sites.

payload
The portion of a frame that contains upper-layer information, such as the user data component.

PCI
Peripheral Component Interconnect. A 32-bit local bus slot that allows the bus direct access to the CPU for devices such as memory and expansion boards and allows the CPU to automat-

ically configure the device using information that is contained on the device.

PDA
personal digital assistant. Stand-alone, hand-held device with computing and communicating abilities.

peripheral device
A device in a computer system that is not part of the core computer system.

phishing
Fraudulent acquisition of sensitive information through the impersonation of a trustworthy source.

ping
A troubleshooting tool used to verify network connectivity by sending a packet to a specific IP address and waiting for the reply.

ping of death
An attack that sent a malformed, malicious, or large pings with the intent to crash the target computer. This type of attack is no longer effective on current computer systems.

pixel
picture element. An element that is the smallest part of a graphic image. Many pixels placed close together make up the image on the computer monitor.

PnP
Plug and Play. Technology that allows a computer to automatically configure the devices that connect to it.

Point of Presence
Point of interconnection between the communication facilities provided by the telephone company and the main distribution facility of the building.

POP3
Post Office Protocol version 3. An application-layer Internet standard that allows a local client to retrieve e-mail from a remote server over a TCP/IP connection.

pop-under
A variation of the popup window advertisement where a new browser window is opened behind the active window making the detection and source more difficult to determine.

popup
A form of online advertising designed to increase web traffic or capture e-mail addresses that displays when a user opens certain websites or clicks on specific links.

popup blocker
Software installed on a computer to block advertisements from displaying.

Post Office Protocol
Standard used to enable access to email messages from a server. Post Office Protocol is often referred to as POP.

power spike
Sudden increase in voltage that is usually caused by lightning strikes.

power supply
Component that converts AC current to DC current used by a computer.

power surge
Increase in voltage significantly above the designated level in a flow of electricity.

Presentation layer
Layer seven of the OSI model. It responds to service requests from the application layer and issues service requests to the session layer.

pretexting
Fraudulent acquisition of sensitive information, primarily over the telephone, where an invented scenario persuades a target of legitimacy.

Print Service
Network service provided for clients that allows access to networked printers.

printer
Output device that produces a paper copy of the information that you create using the computer.

private IP address
IP address that is reserved for internal network use only and cannot be routed on the Internet.

The ranges for IP addresses are 10.0.0.0 to 10.255.255.255, 172.16.0.0 to 172.31.255.255, and 192.168.0.0 to 192.168.255.255.

Protocol stack
Software implementation of a computer networking protocol suite.

prototyping
The process of putting together a working model to test design aspects, demonstrate features, and gather feedback. Prototyping can help reduce project risk and cost.

PSK
pre-shared key. A secret shared between the wireless AP and a client to control access on a network.

PSTN
Public Switched Telephone Network. Wired network that allows telephone calls to be made through both wired and wireless technologies and provides access to the Internet.

public IP address
All IP addresses except those reserved for private IP addresses.

punch down tool
A spring-loaded tool used to cut and connect wires in a jack or on a patch panel.

rack server
Server designed to be installed in an equipment rack.

RADIUS
remote authentication dial in user service. An AAA (authentication, authorization, and accounting) protocol used for security applications, such as network access or IP mobility. It authenticates users and machines in both local and remote situations.

RAM
random access memory. Volatile system memory for the operating software, application programs, and data in current use so that it can be quickly accessed by the computer's processor.

real time
Online at the same time or processed during actual time, not at a later time or date.

receiver
The intended destination for a message through a communication channel.

redirector
An operating system driver that intercepts requests for resources within a computer and analyzes them for remote access requirements. If remote access is required to satisfy the request, the redirector forms a remote-procedure call (RPC) and sends the RPC to lower-layer protocol software for transmission through the network to the node that can satisfy the request.

registered ports
TCP and UDP ports in the range of 1024-49151.

RF
radio frequency. Electromagnetic waves generated by AC and sent to an antenna within the electromagnetic spectrum.

RFC
Request For Comments. A document series used as the primary means to communicate information about the Internet. Most RFCs document protocol specifications such as Telnet and File Transfer Protocol (FTP), but some are humorous or historical. RFCs are available online from numerous sources.

RFI
radio frequency interference. High frequencies that create spikes or noise that interferes with information being transmitted across unshielded copper cabling.

routing
A process to find a path to a destination host. Routing is very complex in large networks because of the many potential intermediate destinations a packet might traverse before reaching its destination host.

routing table
A table stored in router memory, or another internetworking device, that tracks the routes to particular network destinations and, in some cases, metrics associated with those routes to determine where to send data.

RTS
request to send. Along with clear to send, is used by the 802.11 wireless networking protocol to reduce frame collisions introduced by the hidden terminal problem and exposed node problem.

SATA
Serial ATA. A computer bus technology designed for data transfer to and from hard disks and optical drives.

security agent
Software installed on servers and desktop computers that provides threat protection capabilities.

security applicance
Hardware device designed to provide one or more security measures on a network, such as a firewall, intrusion detection and prevention, and VPN services.

security policy
Documentation that details system, physical, and behavioral constraints in an organization.

segment
In a computer network, a portion separated by a computer networking device such as a repeater, bridge, or router. In the OSI model, a PDU at the transport layer.

sender
The source of a transfer of data to a receiver.

server
A computer or device on a network used for network resources and managed by an administrator.

service pack
A collection of updates, fixes, or enhancements to a software program delivered as a single installable package.

Session layer
Layer five of the OSI model. It responds to service requests from the presentation layer and issues service requests to the transport layer.

shell
Software that creates a user interface. A shell provides the user access to the services of the operating system, and to web browsers and e-mail clients.

shorts
An error in a cable caused by low resistance.

site survey
The process of evaluating a network solution to deliver the required coverage, data rates, network capacity, roaming capability, and Quality of Service.

SLA
service level agreement. Contract that defines expectations between an organization and the service vendor to provide an agreed upon level of support.

slammer
A virus that targets SQL servers. Also known as W32.SQLExp.Worm, DDOS.SQLP1434.A, the Sapphire Worm, SQL_HEL, W32/SQLSlammer, and Helkern.

SMTP
Simple Mail Transfer Protocol. Required configuration that allows e-mail to be transmitted over the Internet.

smurf attack
A DoS attack that uses spoofed broadcast ping messages to flood a target computer or network.

social engineering
Techniques used by an attacker to manipulate unsuspecting people into providing information or computer system access.

SOHO
Small Office Home Office. A term used to define the general working environment of small businesses and home based businesses.

sound card
Computer expansion card that enables the input and output sound under control of computer programs.

spam
Unsolicited or junk e-mail messages sent to multiple recipients for either legitimate or fraudulent purposes.

spam filter
Software configured to capture suspicious e-mails before they are sent to a user's in-box.

spoofing
Similar to phishing, a person or program that masquerades as another to gain access to data and the network.

spreadsheet
A table of values arranged in rows and columns of cells used to organize data and calculate formulas.

spyware
A malicious program, typically installed without a user's knowledge or permission, designed to perform tasks such as capture keystrokes, for the benefit of the originator of the program.

spyware protection
A computer application designed to detect and remove spyware.

SSID
service set identifier. The code assigned to a packet that designates that the communication is part of a wireless network.

STA
Abbreviation for STAtion, a basic network device.

Stacheldraht
Malware for Linux and Solaris systems that acts as a DDoS agent to detects and automatically enable source address forgery.

stateful packet inspection
A function of a stateful firewall that distinguishes legitimate packets and allows only those packets that match assigned attributes.

static IP address
An IP address that is not obtained automatically, but is manually configured on a computer.

storage device
Hardware component, such as hard drive, CD drive, DVD drive, tape drive, used to permanently save data.

Streaming audio
Audio content that is continuously received by the end user.

Streaming video
Video content that is continuously received by, and normally displayed to, the end user.

structured cabling system
A uniform cabling system with standards defining the actual cable, cabling distances, type of cable and type of terminating devices.

subnet mask
A 32-bit address mask used in IP to indicate the bits of an IP address that are being used for the subnet address. The second group of numbers in an IP address.

surge protector
Device used to regulate the supplied voltage by blocking or shorting to ground the voltage above a safe threshold.

SYN flooding
A type of DoS attack that sends multiple TCP/SYN packets, often with a forged sender addresses, reducing the ability of the server to respond to legitimate requests.

system requirements
Guidelines that should be met for a computer system to perform effectively.

system resources
Components such as system memory, cache memory, hard disk space, IRQs and DMA channels used to manage applications.

table PC
A type of notebook computer with both a keyboard and an interactive LCD screen able to convert handwritten text into digitized text.

TB
Terabyte. Equal to 1,000 gigabytes

TCO
total cost of ownership. Estimate of direct and indirect costs related to the purchase of computer hardware and software.

TCP
Transmission Control Protocol. Primary Internet protocol for the delivery of data. TCP includes facilities for end-to-end connection establishment, error detection and recovery, and metering the rate of data flow into the network. Many standard applications, such as e-mail, web browser, file transfer, and Telnet, depend on the services of TCP.

TCP/IP model
A layered abstract description for communications and computer network protocol design.

Telnet
Network protocol used on the Internet or a LAN to connect to remote devices for management and for troubleshooting.

TFN
tribe flood network. A set of computer programs that conduct various DDoS attacks such as ICMP flood, SYN flood, UDP flood, and smurf attack.

thick ethernet
An early form of coaxial cable using 10BASE5 for networking. Thick ethernet was once desirable because it could carry signals up to 1640 feet (500 m). Also called thicknet.

thin ethernet
A simple, thin, coaxial network cable for the 10BASE2 system. Thin Ethernet can carry a signal only 607 feet (185 m), but is much easier to work with than thicknet. Also called thinnet.

throughput
The rate at which a computer or network sends or receives data measured in bits per second (bps).

TIA
Telecommunications Industry Association. An organization that develops standards that relate to telecommunications technologies. Together, the TIA and the Electronic Industries Alliance (EIA) have formalized standards, such as EIA/TIA-232, for the electrical characteristics of data transmission.

top down
A troubleshooting technique in a layered concept of networking that starts with the application or highest layer and works down.

traceroute
UNIX/Linux utility that traces the route that a packet takes from source computer to destination host.

trailer
The control information appended to data when data is encapsulated for network transmission.

transmitter
A device used to connect the transmit cable to the network. The transmitter is used to broadcast electromagnetic signals such as radio and television.

Transport layer
Layer four of the OSI model. Responds to service requests from the session layer and issues service requests to the network layer.

Transport protocol
Protocol on the transport layer of the OSI model and TCP/IP reference model used to transfer data on a network.

Trojan horse
A program that appears harmless, but may actually allow hackers to gain access to the computer. Some types of Trojan horses may convince the user to run programs that are damaging to data on the computer.

troubleshooting
A systematic process of eliminating potential causes of a problem used to fix a computer.

unicast
A message sent to a single network destination.

Universal serial bus
An external bus standard that supports a data transfer rate of up to 480 Mbps. A single USB port can be used to connect up to 127 peripheral devices.

UNIX
UNIX is a multi-user, multitasking operating system originally developed in the 1960s and 1970s at Bell Labs. It is one of the most common operating systems for servers on the Internet.

UOM
Units of measurement.

upgrade
The replacement of hardware or software on a computer system with newer hardware or software.

UPS
Backup devices designed to provide an uninterrupted power source in the event of a power failure. They are commonly installed on all file servers.

URL
Uniform Resource Locator. An alpha/numeric string in a specific format that represents a device, file, or web page located on the Internet.

USB
Universal Serial Bus. External serial bus interface standard for the connection of multiple peripheral devices. USB can connect up to 127 USB devices at transfer rates of up to 480 Mbps, and can provide DC power to connected devices.

Vertical application
An application program supporting one specific business process, such as payroll systems or CAD.

Video card
A circuit board plugged into a PC to provide display capabilities.

virtual machine
Technique deployed on servers to enable multiple copies of an operating systems to run on a single set of hardware, thus creating many virtual machines, each one treated as a separate computer. This enables a single physical resource to appear to function as multiple logical resources.

Virtual reality
Technology in which a user interacts with a computer-generated environment.

virtualization
A process that implements a network based on virtual network segments. Devices are connected to virtual segments independent of their physical location and their physical connection to the network.

virus
A self-replicating computer program that spreads by inserting copies of itself into other executable code or documents.

virus scan
Utility that checks all hard drives and memory for viruses.

vishing
Fraudulent acquisition of sensitive information through VoIP that terminates in a computer.

VOD
video on demand. A system enabling a user to watch video on a network.

VoIP
Voice over Internet Protocol. Technology that provides voice over the Internet.

war driving
The act of physically using a vehicle to search for Wi-Fi networks with a laptop or PDA equipped with detection software.

wavelength
The distance between two waves in a repeating pattern.

web hosting
Type of Internet hosting service which includes limited space on a server, used to post websites on the World Wide Web.

well known ports
TCP and UDP ports in the range of 0-1023.

WEP
Wired Equivalent Privacy. Part of the IEEE 802.11 wireless networking standard that provides a low level of security.

WI-Fi
Brand originally licensed by the Wi-Fi Alliance to define the embedded technology of a wireless network, and is based on the IEEE 802.11 specifications.

WiMAX
Worldwide Interoperability for Microwave Access. A standards-based technology enabling the delivery of last mile wireless broadband access as an alternative to cable and DSL.

Windows CE
A version of the Microsoft Windows operating system designed for products such as handheld PCs and other consumer and commercial electronic devices.

Windows Mobile
A compact operating system based on the Microsoft Win32 API that includes a suite of applications designed for mobile devices.

Windows Server
Computer that runs a version of the Microsoft Windows Server operating system.

Windows Vista
The Microsoft operating system after Windows XP, with upgraded security features. The GUI and visual style in Windows Vista are called Windows Aero.

Windows XP
Windows eXPerience. Microsoft operating system that was designed with more stability and user-friendly functionality than previous versions of Windows.

WINS
Windows Internet Naming Service. Microsoft resolution protocol that converts NetBIOS names to IP addresses.

wireless bridge
Physically connects two or more network segments using the 802.11 standard wireless technology in a point-to-point or point-to-multipoint implementation.

wireless client
Any host device that can connect to a wireless network.

WLAN
wireless local area network. Two or more computers or devices equipped to use spread-spectrum technology based on radio waves for communication within a limited area.

Word processor
An application to enable the word processing functions, such as page setup, paragraph and text formatting.

Workstation
A workstation is a PC that is participating in a networked environment. The term has also been used to refer to high-end computer systems for end users. For example, a CAD workstation is typically a powerful computer system with a large monitor suitable for graphics-intensive applications, such as CAD, GIS, and so on.

WPA
Wi-Fi Protected Access. Developed to address security issues in WEP. Provides higher level of security in a wireless network.

WWW
World Wide Web. A large network of Internet servers that provide hypertext and other services to terminals that run client applications such as a web browser.

Yahoo
Internet-based company that provides a search engine, free e-mail, access to news, and links to shopping.

z/OS
A secure IBM 64-bit server operating system that is designed for continuous, high-volume use. z/OS runs Java, supports UNIX and uses TCP/IP.

ZigBee
A suite of high-level communication protocols using small, low-power digital radios based on the IEEE 802.15.4 standard for WPANs. ZigBee operates in ISM radio bands: 868 MHz in Europe, 915 MHz in the U.S., and 2.4 GHz worldwide.

CCNA Discovery
learning resources

Cisco Press, the authorized publisher for the Cisco® Networking Academy®, has a variety of learning and preparation tools to help you master the knowledge and prepare successfully for the CCENT™ and CCNA® exams.

From foundational learning to late-stage review, practice, and preparation, the varied print, software, and video products from Cisco Press can help you with learning, mastering, and succeeding!

Learning Guides

Learning Guides provide the textbook and labs all together as one resource per course.

Networking for Home and Small Business, CCNA Discovery Learning Guide	1587132095 / 9781587132094
Working at a Small-to-Medium Business or ISP, CCNA Discovery Learning Guide	1587132109 / 9781587132100
Introducing Routing and Switching in the Enterprise, CCNA Discovery Learning Guide	1587132117 / 9781587132117
Designing and Supporting Computer Networks, CCNA Discovery Learning Guide	1587132125 / 9781587132124

Other CCENT and CCNA resources

Books, software, and network simulations to help you prepare

31 Days before your CCENT Certification	1587132176 / 9781587132179
31 Days Before your CCNA Exam, Second Edition	1587131978 / 9781587131974
CCNA Official Exam Certification Library, Third Edition	1587201836 / 9781587201837
CCNA Portable Command Guide, Second Edition	1587201933 / 9781587201936
CCNA 640-802 Network Simulator (from Pearson Certification)	1587202166 / 9781587202162
CCNA 640-802 Cert Flash Cards Online	1587202212 / 9781587202216

For more information on this and other Cisco Press products, visit www.ciscopress.com/academy

Cisco Press

Learning is Serious Business. **Invest Wisely.**